C000017862

Sublime
ELEGANCE

The Timeless Charm of Evening Gowns

edited by
VALERIA MANFERTO DE FABIANIS

text by
MARIA MACCARI

editorial staff
LAURA ACCOMAZZO
GIORGIA RAINERI
GIORGIO FERRERO

graphic design
PAOLA PIACCO

Sublime ELEGANCE

The Timeless Charm of Evening Gowns

WHITE STAR PUBLISHERS

CONTENTS

4 Veruschka in a photograph by Horst P. Horst that appeared in *Vogue* in 1966, wearing a palazzo pajama created by the Canadian stylist Arnold Scaasi.

BETWEEN EMOTIONS AND DREAMS

Can an evening gown become a means of seduction? Can it violate the rules and impose a new femininity and new codes of behavior – even before it sets new standards in Haute Couture? Or are we simply deceiving ourselves that this could ever occur, since what women really want is to experience a purely aesthetic pleasure, the eternal dream of seeming to be a fairy tale princess, if only for a moment? There are no certain answers to these questions, but it is clear that what distinguishes an evening gown is its exclusive quality and, at times, its limited accessibility. As its very name implies, an evening gown is to be worn at particular moments and on special occasions. Whether or not it is wearable is not important; what counts is that it transports a woman into another dimension.

"A ball gown must be one of your dreams, and must also make you a dream-like creature," Christian Dior declared in his *Little Dictionary of Fashion*, adding that there must be at least one ball gown in every woman's wardrobe, because it is "so wonderful for morale." There is no doubt that it works wonders for one's morale, even now, a few decades after the great French couturier made the statement, when evening gowns were still a status symbol for women of high social status , when changing for dinner was de rigueur. Things have changed since then. Although this article of clothing in particular has maintained a certain flavor of exclusivity – which imparts a dimension still closely connected to the idea of a dream – at the same time it has undergone a kind of 'democratization'. Consequently, it is not so much those who own an evening gown that lend it its distinctive quality, as the occasions when it is worn. And it is worn less frequently than in the past and is usually confined to two spheres: galas – presentations, various types of festivals, opening night at the theatre and cinema, and charity events –, and more informal evenings – dinner, both out and at home, and art show openings. Only in the former does etiquette still allow dresses that are long or very long, down to the feet or ankles, which in any case should not be worn on less fashionable occasions.

It is no accident that the evening gown is the creation that sets a benchmark for all fashion designers. It is featured in the most important parts of their shows, the final runway walk, which closes an event. And, often, it is the most deluxe number, the one that expresses the essence of their style and also becomes a testing ground where they can experiment with new forms, lines, techniques and materials. However, luxury is not always synonymous with costly material and fabrics and exclusive accessories, even though an evening gown is usually identified with quality fabric such as brocade, velvet, satin, chiffon and taffeta. A black sheath dress that is simple and has common material can do the trick quite well, and many fashion houses offer articles of fine workmanship at very reasonable prices.

Long, very long, or short. Soft or created in almost geometric shapes. Classical or the result of bold experimentation. While evening gowns have eluded canons or codified rules that over time have passed through all sorts of evolution, there is still a thread that connects past and present: the more or less veiled idea of the unattainable and seduction. In other words, something that no woman can do without, when all is said and done.

The Unforgettables

EVENING GOWNS THAT HAVE SHAPED
FASHION HISTORY

Little Black Dress or Petite Robe Noire?

The essential sheath dress, the romantic attire with a wide, puffy skirt, the more sensual slip or siren dresses, or the more androgynous ones such as the *Le Smoking* Tuxedo Dress. There are evening gowns that, more than others, have made their mark on the collective imagination and have helped to shape the history of fashion in various ways. This is because they have helped to codify a new image of women, embodying a dream that has been reproduced again and again, or have allowed women to break free from older ideas while, at the same time, creating a new aesthetic.

One of these was – and still is – the sheath dress or little black dress, which has been seducing both sexes since 1926. Not even now is it showing any signs of going out of fashion. Karl Lagerfeld may have made the most penetrating statement in this regard when he said that "One is never over-dressed or underdressed with a little black dress." And one of this stylist's favorite muses, the former model Inès De La Fressange, even went so far as to consider it not an article of clothing, but rather a 'metaphysical concept', an archetype. In fact, in *Parisian Chic*, she stated that "The little black dress is not an item of clothing, it's a concept. It's abstract, it's universal – which means it's perfect for everyone." There is, perhaps, no article of clothing more versatile and more adaptable to change and variations as the *petite robe noire*, as it is also called: whether short, long, tube or close-fitting, with a high or low neckline, with or without sleeves, with or without a collar – it always lends the wearer an air of chic, elegant and minimal allure. Invented by Coco Chanel in the 1920s, as part of her eternal desire to simplify, convinced as she was that "less is more," this dress was celebrated in 1926 by *Vogue America* as "a sort of uniform for women all over the world, from all backgrounds regardless of their walk of life," thus predicting its success and considering it Mademoiselle Chanel's Ford Model T. And this prediction has proven to be true ever since.

10 Some dresses spark the collective imagination more than others. Among them is the little black dress created by Coco Chanel in the 1920s, which *Vogue American* called "a sort of uniform for women all over the world."

*"If you have the right little black dress,
there is nothing else to wear in its place."*

Wallis Simpson

12 Wallis Simpson, Duchess of Windsor, wearing a long black evening gown.

13 An illustration of two little black dresses designed by Coco Chanel in the 1 April 1927 issue of *Vogue*.

"Fashion is architecture: it is a matter of proportions."

Coco Chanel

14 A silk evening gown with ruche created in 1932 by Coco Chanel and now kept in the Metropolitan Museum of New York.

15 Made in 1936, this seductive black taffeta gown was designed by Chanel and features a close-fitting bodice with a 'now-you-see-it-now-you-don't' effect, a plunging heart-shaped neckline and an ample skirt.

Obviously, black dresses were not new; on the contrary, they were quite common, but they were considered clothing to be worn at funerals, or by women in mourning or by servants. What Chanel did was to liberate them, so to speak, make black, and the black dress, a color and an article for all women which, when combined with the right details and accessories, was suitable for all occasions and at any time, including the evening. "If you have the right little black dress nothing in the world can replace it," stated another woman who was certainly an expert in fashion, Wallis Simpson, the Duchess of Windsor, a passionate collector of the *petite robe noire*. And there must be a good reason why it is still so popular, after all these decades. Suitable for all women and ideal for all occasions, the sheath dress may be one of the items that contributed most to the 'democratization' of fashion in the 20th–century, since this factor was, and still is, intrinsic to its being, above and beyond its economic value or the type of fabric used to make it. This was exactly what Coco Chanel, in her quest for emancipation, had in mind when launching her creation.

The Sheath Dress Becomes the Long Black Dress

Over the years, the little black dress has undergone various minor variations in order to adapt to the times. Examples can be found in movies in which the leading actress playing the role of the femme fatale inevitably wore splendid little black dresses, often long and tight-fitting or with a low neckline. Who can forget the gown that Rita Hayworth wore in *Gilda* (1946)? It was created by the French stylist and Hollywood costume designer Jean Louis, and many think that it is the Evening gown with a capital E. It is certainly one of the most iconic ever, made of black satin, strapless and with a straight neckline, a pencil silhouette and floor-length, with an ample split that goes as far as the thigh. It seems that the stylist drew inspiration from a famous portrait, *Madame X*, by American artist John Singer Sargent.

16 Rita Hayworth in a famous scene from *Gilda* (1946).

17 The long black satin strapless gown with a long, wide slit as worn by Rita Hayworth in *Gilda* (1946), is considered one of the most iconic designs in the history of fashion. It was created by the Hollywood costume designer Jean Louis.

Another version of the little black dress was the design worn by Anita Ekberg in *La dolce vita* (1960): a tantalizing black gown with a very low neckline and wide split. And let us not forget the lovely Audrey Hepburn, wrapped in a legendary black sheath dress designed by Hubert de Givenchy for *Breakfast at Tiffany's* (1961). "She wore a slim cool black dress, black sandals and a pearl choker. [...] A pair of dark glasses blotted out her eyes," Truman Capote wrote in the original novella when describing the protagonist, Holly Golightly, magnificently interpreted in the movie by Hepburn. In that case, the dress was transformed into a long, black, strapless tube made of Italian satin, with a bodice slightly open at the back, a loose floor-length skirt and a wide split at the side. It was accompanied by long gloves and embellished with an elaborate posterior neckline. Not only did it have a great impact on the public at the time, but, since, has never ceased amazing and fascinating people, as, in the meantime, it has become one of those garments that are a symbol of grace and elegance. It is not clear how much the dress owes to Audrey Hepburn or vice versa, but whatever the case, that moment marked the birth of two myths: that of the most slender and elegant actress of all, and that of the iconic, must-have, black tube dress.

18 Actress Anita Ekberg in *La dolce vita* (1960), wearing a tantalizing, long, strapless and figure-hugging sheath dress with a very low, heart-shaped neckline.

19 The famous scene in *La dolce vita* in which Anita Ekberg and Marcello Mastroianni are in the Trevi Fountain. Movie 'femmes fatales' often wore long, tight-fitting and/or low-cut sheath dresses.

*"Givenchy's clothes are the only ones
I feel myself in. He is more than
a designer, he is a creator
of personality."*

Audrey Hepburn

20 Audrey Hepburn as Holly Golightly in the film *Breakfast at Tiffany's* (1961). She is wearing the legendary sheath dress
designed by Hubert de Givenchy, which became a symbol of elegance and style.

21 Made of black Italian satin, floor-length and with a slit, this long dress has a special bateau neckline.

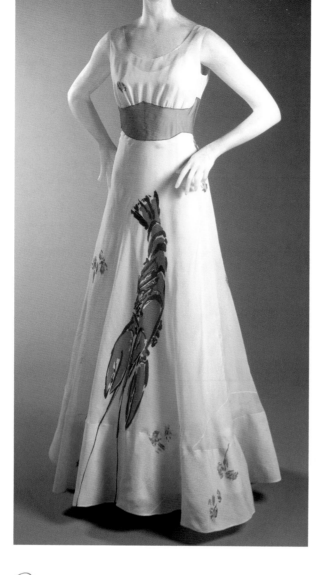

When Art and Fashion Meet: the Lobster Dress

Furthermore, the success of a gown may also depend on many factors, most of which are unfathomable. For example, even a simple lobster can become part of the history of fashion, as the emblem of the link between art and fashion, or better, between the artistic avant-garde and couture. And the lobster in question was the one that surrealist painter Salvador Dalí designed in 1937 and which became translated onto the front of a gown created by stylist Elsa Schiaparelli. Made of white silk etamine, the Lobster Dress was linear, with an A-line skirt and sleeveless bodice with a round neckline. The crustacean occupied the entire front of the skirt, from the waist almost to the ankles, and was even accompanied by sprigs of parsley. Wallis Simpson fell in love with it, and not only did she wear it but she had herself photographed with it while sitting on the ground. Elsa Schiaparelli, whose friends included many of the most popular artists of the time, masters such as Salvador Dalí, Pablo Picasso, Marcel Duchamp and Man Ray, drew inspiration from them for her decidedly original creations, especially her evening gowns. Among these latter, besides the Lobster Dress was the Tears design created by Dalí, in 1938, and made of silk crêpe and with a flowing line.

22 This Elsa Schiaparelli model was made famous by a lobster. It was made in 1937 with étamine white silk, and has an A-shaped skirt and a sleeveless bodice. Wallis Simpson was also enthusiastic about the Lobster Dress.

23 The lobster, surrounded by tufts of parsley, drawn by the Surrealist painter Salvador Dalí.

In the same period, Jean Cocteau decorated an evening mantle for Schiaparelli: bluish-lilac, with a vase of flowers and two women's profiles facing one another, the theme of the double that the poet was developing at the time. The stylist also distinguished herself by inventing highly original accessories. These consisted of hats of all shapes, including a 'shoe hat'; turbans; unusual buttons in the shape of clowns or lips; and finally, a truly fascinating and original object: long gloves with red or gold fingernails. Schiap (as she was known) was also the stylist who colored the world pink; but it was shocking pink, perhaps her most beautiful invention.

24 The poet and dramatist Jean Cocteau was also involved in high fashion. In 1937 he decorated a bluish-lilac mantle designed by Elsa Schiaparelli, creating a flower vase and two faces of women looking at one another: the theme of the double, which was recurrent in his oeuvre.

25 An Elsa Schiaparelli model with a pale purple skirt and a black plissé overskirt that appeared in *Vogue* in 1951. The Italian stylist's creativity also produced a new hue: shocking pink.

26 The Skeleton Dress in black crêpe was designed in 1938 by Salvador Dali together with Schiaparelli for her Circus Collection. Trapunto quilting was used to recreate the spine and ribs.

27 An evening gown that Elsa Schiaparelli designed in 1932. It has a trail, an exposed back, and there is a band around the waist that ends in the back with a spectacular bow.

"Elegance is innate.
It has nothing to do
with being well dressed.
Elegance is refusal."

Diana Vreeland

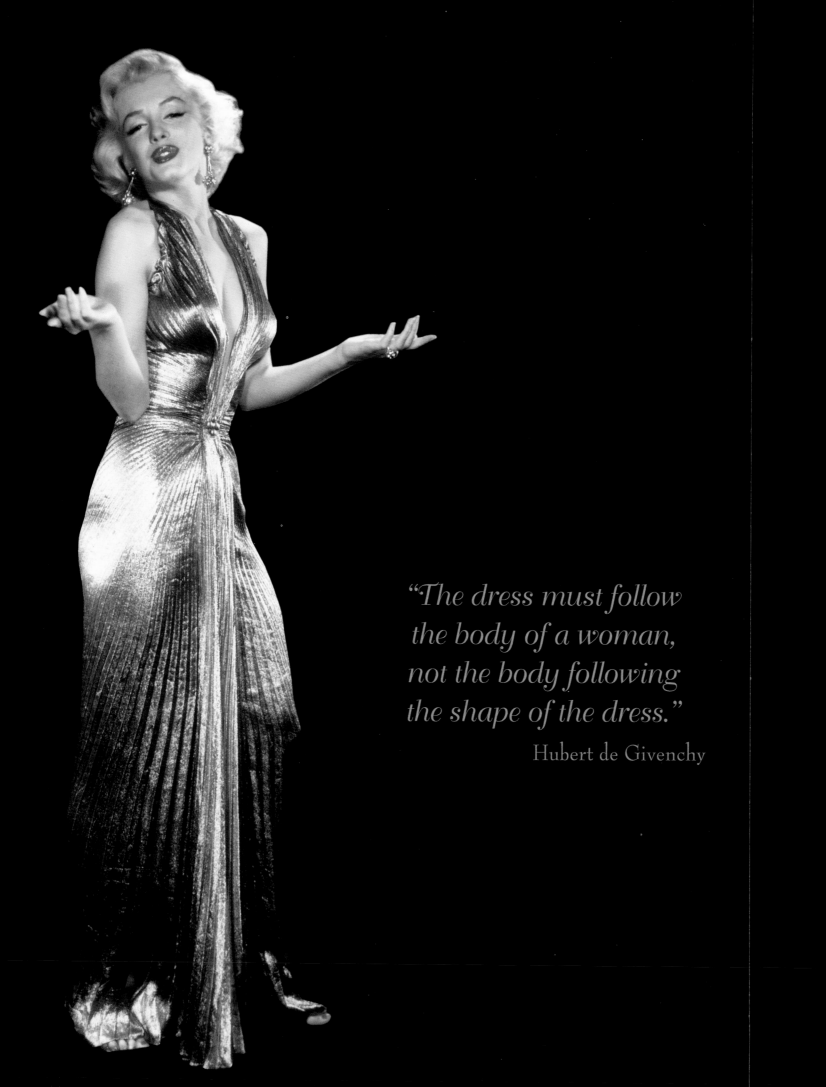

*"The dress must follow
the body of a woman,
not the body following
the shape of the dress."*

Hubert de Givenchy

The Long Dress Becomes Sensual

Shocking pink, or better, fuchsia pink, was also the color of another ankle-length satin gown with a straight neckline: the one Marilyn Monroe immortalized in *Gentlemen Prefer Blondes* (1953). Its line reminded one of Gilda's tube gown, but, unlike the latter, it had a large bow at the back and a narrow belt around the waist. That design, created by American costume designer William Travilla, also includes long gloves. It caused a sensation and was immediately copied. In fact, over 20 years later, the singer Madonna wore a similar dress in her *Material Girl* video. Travilla designed two more evening gowns worn by Marilyn Monroe that also became famous and iconic overnight: the white plissé gown in *The Seven-Year Itch* (1955), and the other one, again pleated but in gold lamé and with a wide V neckline that was also designed for *Gentlemen Prefer Blondes*. All those designs became must-haves and inspired many stylists.

28 Many of the gowns worn by Marilyn Monroe became symbols of sex appeal. Among them was this one, designed by the costume designer William Travilla for *Gentlemen Prefer Blondes* (1953), made of gilded lamé and plissé and with a revealing V neckline.

29 Another iconic dress worn by Marilyn Monroe and designed by William Travilla in 1953: a strapless shocking-pink sheath.

Marilyn Monroe
"7 Year Itch"
Wind scene at Subway

Travilla

30 Marilyn Monroe in the famous scene from *The Seven Year Itch* (1955). This white pleated gown became one of the most famous and most imitated.

31 A drawing of the same dress, which William Travilla designed in 1952.

Marilyn Monroe also wore another memorable gown, on 19 May 1962, during the celebration of President Kennedy's 45th birthday at Madison Square Garden. And, as if that special "Happy birthday, mister President" were not enough to make the atmosphere even more 'spicy', there was the gown that she wore: flesh colored and so tight it was like a second skin that made her seem to be naked. It was created by costume designer Jean Louis, and is obviously considered one of the most enticing and sexy evening gowns in the history of fashion. The color and form were further enhanced by the fact that it was off-the-shoulder and backless, had a plunging neckline and small embroidered strass rosettes that heightened the texture of the very thin fabric, which had come from a French silk factory and was as impalpable as a cobweb. Closed by a very thin zip and tiny hooks, it was so audacious that the stylist remarked, "Only Marilyn Monroe would have had the courage to wear it." At the time, it was said that it had been sewn directly onto her body and that she wore no underclothing. (The gown, which at the time cost 2500 USD, was later sold at Christie's for an eye-watering 1,267,500 USD, the most expensive dress ever.) What is certain is that it was much appreciated by the person it was intended for, the President, who exclaimed, "I can now retire from politics after having had *Happy Birthday* sung to me in such a sweet, wholesome way." Over the years, many celebrities have shown off bold gowns while parading on red carpets, but no one has managed to rouse such strong feelings with such grace and elegance, as Marilyn Monroe.

32 The flesh-colored marquisette gown created by Hollywood costume designer Jean Louis for Marilyn Monroe, who wore it on 19 May 1962 on the occasion of President Kennedy's 45th birthday.

33 Jean Louis's gown was so figure-hugging that Monroe seemed to be nude. This effect was also created by the exposed back and the décolleté, as well as the shape and color. It is still considered one of the most tantalizing evening dresses ever made.

The Bon Chic of Two Icons: Jackie and Grace

While on the subject of female icons connected to personages, mention must be made of two women who left their mark on fashion for decades: Jackie Kennedy and Grace Kelly, symbols of the aristocratic fascination and bon ton typical of stylist Oleg Cassini, who was responsible their 'sartorial destiny'. Two women with a different charisma and temperament, and two looks that seemed to be similar but were really distinct. Cassini made Jackie his muse, designing the dresses that she wore as First Lady, influencing the image of an entire decade, the 1960s. Cassini created the famous evening dress she wore during an official visit to France, when, standing with Charles De Gaulle, President Kennedy uttered a phrase that went down in history: "I am the man who accompanied Jacqueline Kennedy to Paris." An equally iconic gown was the one Cassini designed for the Inauguration Gala in 1961, of which he said, "It was long, of geometric simplicity, spare except for a French cockade at the waist. I described to Jackie the tone the new Administration would acquire. And John was very proud of her look." The message was quite clear: simplicity and elegance, that of a traditional bon ton style that was modernized and rejuvenated, based on solid sartorial experience and skill and quality fabrics. The 300 or so gowns he designed for her had straight, geometric lines, in particular in an Empire or tube style. The colors were always delicate, preferably pastel, and such details and decorative elements as brooches, bows and flowers were applied discreetly to enliven the rest of the gown.

34 Jackie Kennedy in 1961, seated next to Soviet Premier Nikita Khrushchev and wearing a long white gown created by Oleg Cassini.

35 President Kennedy during the Inauguration Gala beside the extremely elegant Jackie, who is wearing a sophisticated evening dress with a French cockade at her waist designed for her by Cassini.

The look of the other woman who marked the career, as well as the private life, of Oleg Cassini – Grace Kelly – was slightly different. The actress and stylist hit it off immediately, and their muse-master relationship bloomed into a romantic tie that ended when Grace decided to marry Prince Rainier. Ironically enough, the gown the future princess wore when she first met Rainier had been designed by Cassini. "I created a Grace Kelly look: elegant but restrained dresses," Cassini said.

36 Grace Kelly and Oleg Cassini. The actress and the stylist had a close relationship that was both professional and private.

37 Grace Kelly, wearing a Cassini evening dress in this 1955 photograph shot by Erwin Blumenfeld.

The New Look: the Birth of the Corolla Dress

There are tube, slip, close-fitting and siren dresses, without neglecting the most classic of all, the one that in the collective imagination is associated most with the concept of the 'dream': the ball gown with a voluminous skirt, elegant decoration, and a bodice that emphasizes the form of the bust and is often off-the-shoulder.

Without doubt, one of the most famous ball gowns was the Paris Dress that Grace Kelly wore in Alfred Hitchcock's *Rear Window* (1954). It was designed by American costume designer and stylist Edith Head, along with five other designs for the film. But the black and white one that the protagonist's girlfriend Lisa Fremont wore on her return to Paris, is the most famous. The reason why a gown remains impressed in the collective imagination more than others is a mystery, a strange alchemy made of suggestions that are perhaps so striking because they reflect the spirit of the moment. And the destiny of the ball gown lies in this, because the full line of the skirt, made of layers of chiffon and tulle, influenced by the ballerina style and decorated, in the upper part, with black tree branches, seems to fully embody the spirit of the New Look. The upper part of the dress has a black bodice with a V neckline on the back, a décolleté and short sleeves. Rounding it off are a chiffon stole, long white gloves and a black patent leather belt around the waist.

38 and 39 Grace Kelly wearing the Paris Dress, a ball gown created by costume designer Edith Head
for *Rear Window* (1954). This gown is the perfect embodiment of the New Look spirit that prevailed in this period,
made of tulle chiffon and with a tight-fitting black bodice with a V neckline.

Another black and white gown enchanted the female public and became one of the most iconic garments in the history of fashion: the ball gown that Audrey Hepburn wore in *Sabrina* (1954). Designed by Hubert de Givenchy, it was ankle-length, sleeveless, a tube with embroidered black flowers, topped in the back by a full organdy corolla skirt. The gown was often imitated and it marked the beginning of the collaboration and friendship between Givenchy and Audrey Hepburn. After that, he created her most important designs, those that earned him worldwide fame and made her the icon of a unique and timeless style. "His are the only clothes in which I feel myself. He is far more than a couturier, he is a creator of personality," the actress said.

40 Audrey Hepburn in *Sabrina* (1954) wearing an evening dress designed by Hubert de Givenchy:
a sheath skirt with an ample organza overskirt in the back.

"I think that dresses with voluminous skirts have a more romantic air," Christian Dior suggested in his *Little Dictionary of Fashion*. Christian Dior was the one who, after World War Two, introduced the so-called corolla style, which gave rise to the most formal garment, the one classified as a 'ball gown' to be worn only on special occasions. It was also the one that drew most from the past, from 19th-century crinoline and even from skirts that were very wide at the hips and so popular in the 18th-century, which the creator of the New Look revived and modernized in his Corolla collection, presented to the public on 12 February 1947 and immediately hailed as revolutionary by the press.

42 Christian Dior, the inventor of the New Look, in his atelier, putting the finishing touches to a dress.

43 Dior observing a model wearing a splendid red corolla evening dress that he designed.

"When wearing a ball gown one feels like a real woman, all femininity, grace and delicacy."

Christian Dior

44 An illustration of a New Look style dress that Dior created in 1948.

45 Christian Dior's May Dress (1953), made of silk with floral embroidery.

46 Dior's Junon Dress, part of the 1949-50 fall-winter collection: silk with overlaid flounces and richly decorated with variously colored sequins.

47 Christian Dior's Venus Dress, part of the 1949-50 fall-winter collection: silk decorated with sequins, paillettes, beads and pearls.

In the United States, high society turned to the Anglo-American stylist Charles James, who was a visionary who had a great impact on sartorial technique. In 2014, the Metropolitan Museum of Art held a retrospective show featuring his extraordinary designs, whose names alone give us an idea of their elegant lightness: Swan, Clover Leaf, Butterfly, and Tree. What was amazing about his work was his scientific, mathematical, and engineering-like approach to design, words that we find it hard to associate with the idea of a dream. Yet James succeeded in transforming what was apparently an antithesis into a synthesis, producing such unique creations as the Clover Leaf.

48 Two evening gowns created in 1950 by the great American couturier Charles James.

49 Mrs. Howard Reilly wearing a dress designed by James, who is standing beside her.

51 The Butterfly Dress (1955) by Charles James. Like so many other models by this stylist, this is a very elaborate creation, consisting of a huge amount of fabric or silk skillfully distributed to heighten its elegance to the utmost.

52 and 53 The sculptural Swan Dress that Charles James designed in 1954.

"*Everyone turns when I sweep into the room [wearing a James creation]: the gentlemen in admiration, the ladies in envy.*"

Austine Hearst

The Revolution in Form

The protagonist of a true revolution in the construction of evening dress was the Spaniard Cristóbal Balenciaga, who, more than a stylist, can be considered an artist with great sartorial skill and experience combined with unique creative inventiveness and a capacity for innovation that few great fashion designers could boast. Christian Dior said that Balenciaga was "the couturier of couturiers, the master of us all." He was official tailor to the Spanish court as well as to the aristocracy and bourgeoisie of the time, a very select and exclusive clientele. Unlike Dior or James, Balenciaga did not create showy and luxurious garments, but spare, elegant and linear attire, which led Coco Chanel to exclaim, "Balenciaga is a true couturier. Only he is able to cut fabric, assemble it and sew it with his own hands. The others are merely draftsmen." That statement alone would be enough to place him in the pantheon of fashion and art. His approach to fashion design was also unique and contrary to that of the other two stylists. He eliminated all the trappings, placing his emphasis on the body the dress had to adapt to, and fit, in order to lend it the most freedom of movement. "A beautiful dress follows the body, and only the body," he used to say, and, in fact, his work and production were based on that principle, which he set out to realize with continual experimentation and innovation. He worked constantly and intensely with fabrics, even going so far as to have one created especially for

54 A model wearing a long pink velvet gown with a belt around the waist and a soft bodice, designed by Balenciaga.

55 Cristóbal Balenciaga created soft and elegant patterns on the human body.

him: gazar, a rather rigid silk that retains its shape and was thus ideal for his evening gowns. Carrying on the work of Madame Vionnet, the only other fashion designer who could be compared to him for inventiveness and creativity, Balenciaga believed that clothing had to make women beautiful regardless of their size. Indeed, it is said that he actually preferred women who were somewhat plump because they enhanced his lines and volumes, which were extremely innovative and always a step ahead of designs created by other stylists. In 1951, he created a line of hourglass, black velvet garments that were inspired by Spain and by flamenco; the lower part of the gown was raised in front and ended at the back with a small train, revealing a contrasting fabric both in texture and in color. In 1955, he created a tunic line and, two years later, the 'sack dress', which he invented with his pupil of the time, Hubert de Givenchy, which entailed the 'disappearance' of the waistline and which skimmed over the forms of the body almost without touching them, as in the Baby Doll dress created in 1958, influenced by children's clothing and affording total freedom to the wearer. "Oh, those collections! Never before had we seen such colors, such purples!" Diana Vreeland exclaimed in her autobiography. And it was not only purples, because yellows, pinks and corals were also used to add an extra touch to the exquisite fabrics and cuts, in blocks of contrasting colors, at times to liven up a black or one-color dress by adding a simple, brightly colored stole. Again, referring to Balenciaga, Diana Vreeland stated: "He was the greatest stylist who ever existed. If a woman came in in a Balenciaga dress, no other woman in the room existed. Balenciaga often said that women did not have to be perfect or beautiful to wear his clothes. When they wore his clothes, they became beautiful."

56 Three models wearing Balenciaga creations in a 1951 image that drew inspiration from paintings by Henri de Toulouse-Lautrec.

57 Balenciaga used color, either in blocks or in contrasting hues such as black and yellow, to highlight fabrics and simple lines even more.

58 Princess Irene Galitzine wearing one of her famous palazzo pajama designs.

59 A model in the Galitzine 2013 spring-summer collection.

The Palazzo Pajama and the Tuxedo Trousers Conquer the Evening

An evening gown can be a weapon of seduction as well as a means of breaking all the rules and imposing a new type of femininity. Trousers, for example, appeared on the Haute Couture scene in 1960 thanks to Irene Galitzine, who created the so-called palazzo pajama: a two-piece suit, blouse and pants that are more or less puffy, of an unmistakable sartorial stamp and usually made of silk with the hems sometimes decorated with beads, fringes and strass. That evening attire immediately conquered the aristocrats, the jet setters and the actresses, including true icons of style such as Marella Agnelli and Jacqueline Kennedy, who sent a special letter of thanks to Galitzine, calling the gift a 'pajama' and adding that she liked it very much. The name is attributed to Diana Vreeland, who was so enthusiastic about the new model that she wrote an entire article on it that appeared in *Vogue USA*. The setting was the Brazilian Embassy in the Palazzo Doria Pamphilij in Piazza Navona, Rome, and the gown was worn not by professional models, but by members of the Italian aristocracy who were friends of the princess-stylist.

*"My favorite creation is the
palazzo pajama because it was
the beginning of my success."*

Irene Galitzine

And Galitzine's new 'suits' were designed for formal receptions held in her home, and were so richly decorated that they made one compare it more to a sumptuous palace rather than a simple house. The palazzo pajama became famous in a very short time and even won the Fashion Oscar that very year, 1960. Some examples are kept in three of the most important museums in the world, the Metropolitan Museum of Art in New York, the Victoria and Albert Museum in London and the Museum of Costumes in St. Petersburg. In 2013, stylist Sergio Zambon paid a tribute to the palazzo pajama with an entire collection.

60 Princess Irene Galitzine surrounded by models wearing some of her gowns.

61 With her palazzo pajama creations Galitzine won the 1960 Fashion Oscar. Some of them are kept in the most important museums in the world.

But the true revolution in evening gowns arrived in 1966 thanks to Yves Saint Laurent, who introduced typically masculine features into women's garments. In a famous statement, Pierre Bergé, his life-long partner, said that "Chanel gave women freedom. Yves Saint Laurent gave them power." He also gave them a 'uniform' that epitomized their values while retaining all the allure and mystery of femininity: the Tuxedo Dress, men's evening dress par excellence, adapted for the female body. The original version was presented in the 1966 Pop Art collection and consisted of a black dinner jacket with satin cuffs, a white shirt with ruches, a black bow tie and slim-line trousers with satin strips on the sides. The stylist proposed the Tuxedo Dress as alternative evening attire to the classic little black dress and it immediately had a tremendous impact. Imagine an evening suit 'stolen' from a man's wardrobe, or better, from codified men's formal evening wear at the time: for a woman, wearing this and showing it off was a way of being irreverent, transgressive and feminist.

Besides Galitzine, other stylists like Paul Poiret and Chanel had already designed trousers for women, but they were more like slacks, wide and fluid, and were certainly not meant to be worn as evening dress. And many movie actresses – Greta Garbo, Marlene Dietrich, Katharine Hepburn, for example – had worn men's suits. But the novelty of Yves Saint Laurent's creation was that he liberated the tuxedo, so to speak, by making it a part of a collection, and above all by creating other designs of *Le Smoking* almost every season afterwards. It was slightly modified in the form, details, colors and style, but has remained popular to this day. It seems that inspiration came to the stylist from the clothes worn by the avant-garde artist Niki de Saint Phalle, who often wore men's suits with high heels. The tuxedo became an immediate hit with movie stars and was especially admired by Catherine Deneuve, Lauren Bacall and Liza Minnelli. Bianca Jagger was so enthusiastic that she wore it for her wedding in 1972, and also made it a sort of personal uniform, wearing many variations of it. To this day, there is no movie star who has not worn it as evening attire at least once. Angelina Jolie wore one designed by Hedi Slimane for Saint Laurent at the 2014 Bafta Awards. But why this long-lasting love for a garment that is apparently rather un-feminine? Yves Saint Laurent himself offered the explanation that this success was due mostly to sartorial details, an attitude, and a way of acting when he said, "For a woman, le *smoking* is an indispensable garment with which she finds herself continually in fashion, because it is about style, not fashion. Fashions come and go, but style is forever."

63 Yves Saint Laurent with Catherine Deneuve, one of his muses, together with a mannequin wearing a Tuxedo Dress, the most 'revolutionary' stylistic invention of this great couturier.

64 A model displaying the Tuxedo Dress suit. Saint Laurent proposed it as alternative evening attire to the classical black sheath, and it enjoyed immediate success, making a great impact on the fashion world.

65 In the 2002 spring-summer show Yves Saint Laurent said farewell to catwalks with a collection celebrating his most iconic models, one of which was the Tuxedo Dress.

"A girl should be two things: classy and fabulous."

Coco Chanel

The Travolta Style: Famous for One Night

Then there are gowns that became famous overnight. An illustrious example is Lady Diana's Travolta Dress, a dark blue velvet evening gown that she wore during her first official visit to the United States, in 1985. But why the name Travolta? Because actor John Travolta danced with the princess during a gala at the White House, and Diana, a guest of President Reagan and the First Lady, was wearing the gown. This caused such a sensation that the gown remained in the collective imagination, becoming the very symbol of that trip. And the symbol of one of the few carefree moments Lady Diana enjoyed. The gown was designed by Victor Edelstein, the stylist who had created many of Diana's ball gowns before her divorce, and who was considered the English equivalent of Oscar de la Renta. It drew inspiration from the Edwardian period with its S line and its fabric, a truly royal velvet. The photographs of Travolta and Lady Diana dancing were immediately seen throughout the world, and the gown was instantly dubbed the Travolta Dress. Afterwards, Diana wore it on two other official occasions, in Germany in 1987 and at the premiere of *Wall Street* (1987). And then one final time in 1997, a few months before her death, in the last official photograph of her taken by Lord Snowdon. But no one remembers those other occasions, given the overwhelming impression the gown had made while floating and flowing in the White House ballroom, worn by a happy princess.

66 The dark blue velvet gown designed by Victor Edelstein in 1985 and worn by Lady Diana during her first official visit to the United States.

67 The Travolta Dress was named after the gown the princess wore while dancing with actor John Travolta at the White House.

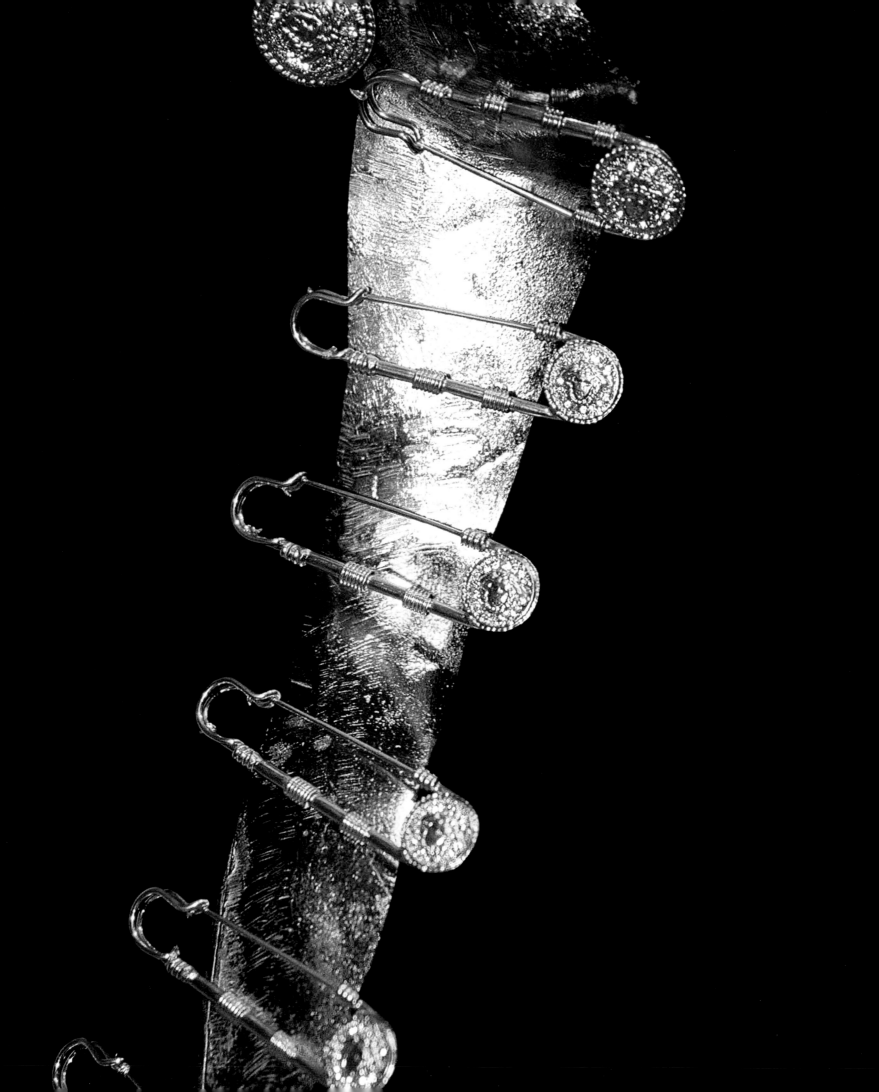

Slits and Safety Pins

Few other gowns can equal the success enjoyed by Lady Diana's. Certainly one of the most famous of these is Versace's black gown with safety pins that brought fame, practically overnight, in 1994 to an almost unknown model, Elizabeth Hurley, who wore it at the premiere of the movie *Four Weddings and a Funeral* (1994). And, naturally, the person who designed it, Gianni Versace, became famous too. Why did this gown have such an impact on the media? Because it was certainly different from all the others up to that time, and because it was in the right place at the right time. Sensual, even brazen, and undoubtedly audacious, it left very little to the imagination and seemed to have been created expressly to be noticed. And this is what Hurley herself must have thought when she decided to wear it that evening. Made of silk and Lycra, extremely figure-hugging but, as if that were not enough, literally held together by several gilded safety pins in strategic points to connect the front and back of the gown while leaving much of the hips and thighs exposed to view. Obviously, everyone talked about it and, to this day, the dress is perhaps Versace's best-known creation, still remembered as one of the most beautiful of all time. Filled with "neo-punk influences and something that recalls the sari," as the stylist himself admitted, it could be considered a sensual version of the classic little black dress, an evolution that mirrors women's role at the time, that is, in the early 1990s. In 2012, Lady Gaga paid tribute to this iconic garment by wearing it at a gala in Milan.

68 Detail of the audacious gown, made of silk and Lycra and with safety pins, designed in 1994 by Gianni Versace.

69 This evening dress became famous overnight after it was worn by the then unknown Elizabeth Hurley.

"My objective is to help women become the best version of themselves."

Tom Ford

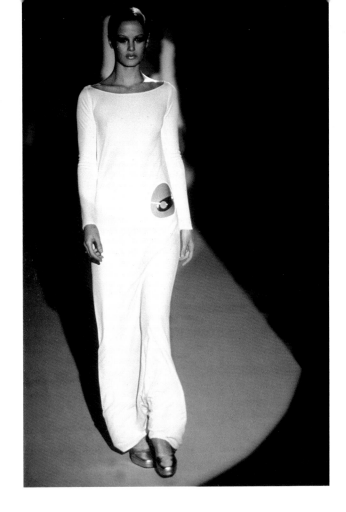

The Emergence of Minimal Chic

And how about combining minimalism and sensuality? The Texan stylist Tom Ford made the combination of these two elements his very own style as well as the style of Gucci, where he was creative director from 1990 to 2004. It was the 1996-1997 fall-winter collection that marked the peak of Tom Ford's artistic vision while he was with Gucci, the collection that embodies all its values. The white columnar dresses, in particular, represent the synthesis of this, and are also the 'manifesto' of an entire decade, marked by minimalism in both form and color. Ankle-length, and made of jersey, and not at all close-fitting, with their white color these dresses seem to be in contrast with this lingering over form, caressing without constricting and indicating curves without emphasizing them. The touch of glamor is provided by the strategically located splits, on the hips and the abdomen, again suggesting a sensuality that is never audacious. These cuts are embellished with metal elements, accompanied by laces that hold up the plunging necklines that descend to the pelvis. This is a reference to certain 1970 glam influences, expressed by stylists like Halston and by his glittering tube dresses.

70 A white Gucci gown designed by Tom Ford for the 1996-1997 fall-winter collection.

71 Made of ankle-length white jersey cloth, this model is the essence of Tom Ford's style: elegant and minimal and yet extremely sexy, partly thanks to the strategically placed cutouts on the hips and midriff.

When a Color Determines the Style

How much does the color of a garment contribute to its success? Can a color become as iconic as a design, and even embody an entire style and its creator? Well, this is precisely what happened to Valentino and his red, his famed Valentino Red, a very special nuance of this color. It is a bright shade tending toward orange, which it seems the stylist discovered during a trip to Spain in the 1950s, in particular to Barcelona, where, while watching a play in which the actors wore costumes whose red color was so amazing, and so overwhelming, he became ecstatic and imagined that the stage was a catwalk. The 2013 spring-summer Haute Couture collection was a kind of tribute to his spectacular career and, naturally, included 'Valentino Red' garments. Equally spectacular was the exhibition, in 2007, at the Ara Pacis in Rome to celebrate the maestro's 45-year career.

72 The stylist Valentino photographed in 2007 at the Ara Pacis in Rome with some of his historic creations, during the show celebrating his 45-year career.

73 White and red Valentino gowns on display at the Ara Pacis. The color red became his special stylistic feature and an icon of high fashion.

74 A Valentino gown shown at the 2013 Haute Couture spring-summer collection. It was designed by Maria Grazia Chiuri and Pierpaolo Piccioli, the heirs of the Maison Valentino.

75 Detail from one of the designs in the collection, made of macramé lace in the shade created by and named after the great Italian stylist, Valentino red.

A Question of Balance

DETAIL THAT SEDUCES

The Neckline, the True Essence of an Evening Gown

The neckline is the component that, even more than length and slits, most distinguishes an evening dress, for which, let's admit it, everything is forgiven in the name of glamor, sensual allure and that famous 'dream effect' that, to some degree, represents its essence. As regards sartorial construction and balance, and effectively above and beyond color, line, cut and decorations, often it is a well-modulated and positioned neckline that imparts a particular twist to a gown that might otherwise have little impact or even be nondescript, thus making it intriguing and sexy.

It all began with *Les Merveilleuses* in the early 1800s, the women that Napoleon chastised because of their excessive nudity, their clothes with high waistlines, barely visible short sleeves, and very small bodices that barely covered their breasts, women who understood the power of seduction that a well-displayed neckline could unleash. This sensuality smacked strongly of liberation from the revolution that had just ended and everything it represented. The flappers in the 1920s also wore sleeveless dresses with a straight line that were accompanied by gloves that went up to the elbow; and it was even better if the young woman had rather small breasts, because the garments could then flow and fall without any 'obstacle'. In this case, the neckline was not the most important part of dressing up: it was the length of the garment that attracted all the attention as, for the first time, it was a bit more than knee-length.

78 Grace Kelly, in a 1954 photograph, wearing an evening gown with a heart-shaped neckline,
perfect for highlighting the shoulders and arms.

This underwent an abrupt change in the following decade, when the exposed backs and plunging necklines of the new goddesses of Hollywood greatly influenced the taste of the period by making its overwhelming entrance into the collective imagination of both men and women, especially the former. The stars were wrapped in siren dresses, which Madame Vionnet had perfected with the invention of the bias cut. They were made of satin and other very soft fabrics, often with light colors from white to the neutral beige and greys of those designed by Adrian for Joan Crawford, and in the long gowns worn by Jean Harlow.

80 The model Sonia Colmer wearing a dress with a halterneck designed by Madeleine Vionnet in 1938. This neckline is ideal for bringing out ample shoulders.

81 The stylist Madeleine Vionnet invented the bias cut, which created various panels that were draped around the body and showed it off to perfection.

82 Nude backs and low necklines strongly influenced esthetic taste in the 1930s and 1940s thanks to fluttering light dresses made of such fluid fabrics as chiffon and crêpe de Chine that cling to the body, highlighting its curves in a natural manner.

83 The diagonal cut allowed the fabric to adhere perfectly to the silhouette, the drapery flowing down to the feet in loose folds without any need for pleats on the hips to create the shape of the skirt.

"*The dress must not hang on the body but follow its lines. It must accompany its wearer, and when a woman smiles the dress must smile with her.*"

Madeleine Vionnet

84 The great costume designers who worked for the movie studios created Hollywood glamor. One of the most famous was Adrian, who designed clothes for almost all the great stars, from Greta Garbo to Katharine Hepburn and Norma Shearer.

85 Adrian designed unforgettable long dresses for Joan Crawford, the actress with whom he had a special relationship, even creating shoulder pads for her.

86 This magnificent plissé dress with halterneck was created by the costume
designer Adrian and worn by Joan Crawford in *Susan and God* (1940).

87 Often, a well-proportioned and well-tailored neckline lends a special twist to a
dress that would otherwise be nondescript, imparting an intriguing and sexy look.

"You can have anything you want in life if you dress for it."

Edith Head

88 and 89 One of the most glamorous stars in the heyday of Hollywood was the 'platinum blonde' Jean Harlow, whose sex appeal led to a new type of femininity and new clothing styles, for example, the slip dress. Ankle-length slip dresses often exposed the back and had a low neckline.

A crucial contribution was made by another great couturier, Elsa Schiaparelli, who in the 1930s invented the one-shoulder neckline, which was asymmetrical and so tantalizing that it was named after the goddess of hunting, Diana. And, at the 2006 Metropolitan Museum Gala, actress Sarah Jessica Parker wore a design with a one-shoulder neckline, created by Alexander McQueen.

Without a doubt, the emblem of what, in the collective imagination, is considered the most seductive and unrivalled evening gown, is a long strapless design with a low neckline. The mythical fascination of bare shoulders is best represented in what is perhaps the most iconic evening gown of all, the black one worn by Rita Hayworth in *Gilda* (1946), while in *To Catch a Thief* (1955) Grace Kelly displays a series of extremely elegant gowns, including the famous design in light blue with a straight neckline worn in the scene where she tries to seduce Cary Grant, and the other strapless ice-white gown with a heart-shaped neckline.

90 Two Elsa Schiaparelli models in a 1934 drawing by Rene Bouet-Willaumez.

90-91 Elsa Schiaparelli wearing a sumptuous dress with a one-shoulder neckline that she invented, asymmetrical and so enticing that it was named after the goddess of hunting Diana.

92 The most seductive evening gown in the collective imagination is the long dress with a strapless neckline.
Here we see Grace Kelly in *To Catch a Thief* (1955).

93 Grace Kelly in the film *To Catch a Thief* wearing a magnificent light blue chiffon columnar gown created
by the costume designer Edith Head.

On the other hand, some stylists, aware of the power that a strategically placed neckline could wield, searched for and experimented with new solutions and creations. One of these was Oleg Cassini, who studied a variation of the strapless straight neckline for Jackie Kennedy, the so-called cuff. What he did was to double the strip of fabric covering the breasts in Empire style garments or ball gowns, a formula that was soon widely adopted, even for wedding dresses. Necklines alone have often made certain gowns immortal. One of these is the black tube dress, designed by Hubert de Givenchy and worn by Audrey Hepburn in *Breakfast at Tiffany's* (1961), which featured a bateau neckline in front and a geometric neckline in the back. Another gown, again black, and again with a bateau neckline and an almost totally exposed back, was designed by Christian Dior for Marilyn Monroe and was immortalized in a Bert Stern photograph a mixture of seductiveness and innocence. Monroe loved 'maxi necklines', either plunging or straight. Some dresses that she wore on set immediately became famous, such as the gold pleated gown in *Gentlemen Prefer Blondes* (1953) which had an audacious, plunging American neckline.

94 Oleg Cassini studied a variation of the straight, strapless neckline for Jackie Kennedy: the strip of fabric that covers the breasts in Empire garments or ball gowns was doubled, thus creating the 'cuff dress'.

95 Some of the best-known dresses worn by the First Lady were designed by Oleg Cassini.

"Elegance must be the right combination of distinction, naturalness, care and simplicity."

Christian Dior

97 Marilyn Monroe, photographed by Berte Stern, wearing a seductive model designed by Christian Dior, with a plunging neckline on her back.

The décolleté later became the favorite area of experimentation for Jean Paul Gaultier, who sparked a mini-revolution in the sartorial world by setting the *guêpiere* or torsolette in the limelight, underscoring the seductive role this part of a dress could play. The quintessence of a beguiling undergarment, it was taken from its hiding place in the bureau and transformed into an iconic accessory and even an integral part of the evening gown. In fact, in 1984, Gaultier created a velvet dress with a cone bra, the symbol of intriguing, self-assured femininity, the same one he used when designing the costumes for Madonna's 1990 Blonde Ambition Tour, which made the cone corset one of the most legendary items in the history of fashion.

98 Madonna during her 1990 Blonde Ambition Tour, wearing the iconic silk corset with a 'cone bra' designed by Jean Paul Gaultier. From that moment on, underwear began to be used as an accessory for evening attire.

99 One of the sketches by Jean Paul Gaultier of the costumes worn during Madonna's 1990 tour.

From that moment, lingerie in general was 'liberated' and made popular, partly thanks to the work of Italian fashion duo Dolce & Gabbana. Bustiers and bras, often associated with lace and hourglass lines, and slip dresses of Sicilian inspiration in such fine fabrics as lace, which was often black, became their iconic creation and their on-going stylistic feature and it was present in all their subsequent collections. As their 'muse', they chose model and actress Monica Bellucci, who was featured in many of their publicity campaigns and personified their seductive style with a touch of retro. This fashion suddenly burst onto the scene in the 1980s, in a world of career women with its simple, spare look defined by exponents of minimalism such as the Americans Calvin Klein and Donna Karan and the Italian stylist Giorgio Armani.

100 Monica Bellucci epitomizes the ideal of femininity and the essence of style created by the fashion designer duo Dolce & Gabbana: an enticing woman with a touch of retro.

101 Bustiers and bras are the iconic creations of Dolce & Gabbana, often together with lace and hourglass attire.

This minimalism greatly influenced the vocabulary of fashion designer Tom Ford, whose remarkable marriage of sensuality and elegance, achieved through the masterful and calculated use of cuts, splits and necklines, never fails to be unpredictable and surprising. Indeed, his creations are distinguished for their vein of glamor, and models such as those featured in the historic Collezione Bianca (White Collection), which he designed for Gucci in 1996, created a trend. These designs are columnar, made of matte jersey fabric and with long and revealing slits and holes over the entire bust whose seductive effect is counterbalanced by the line and the white color. They remind one of the garments designed by another American stylist, Roy Halston, who made seduction his strong point in the 1970s, with his soft dresses that caressed the body, and whose back and décolleté were exposed in order to highlight the femininity of an intriguing, sophisticated woman.

102 A long chiffon dress with pastel hues and a plunging V neckline designed by Roy Halston in 1975
and worn by the model Beverly Johnson.

103 A seductive dress from the Gucci Collezione Bianca, designed in 1996 by Tom Ford, a columnar jersey with
a plunging neckline and deep folds that cross over the entire bust.

104 Two Valentino models: the first one with a straight neckline held on the breast by a knot,
and the other a jersey with a one-shoulder neckline.

*"Elegance
is the balance
between proportion,
emotion
and surprise."*

Valentino

Finally, there is the back, and the subtle fascination and power this part of the body can exert if properly set in the foreground by rather broad and low necklines. This is something even Chanel introduced in some of her designs, the first little, soft, black dresses, like a classical black made of silver and black silk designed in 1931, and other dresses with a more siren line that were created in the same period. One of her contemporaries, Madeleine Vionnet, used her iconic elements, knots, by placing them right on the upper part of the back. However, the gown that Hilary Swank wore at the 2005 Academy Awards – a long blue dress created by Guy Laroche that exposed her entire back as far as the lumbar region – was simply unsurpassable and became an overnight sensation. Ironically, the front was quite 'proper', with a high neckline and long sleeves. And if, as Givenchy stated, "the dress must follow the woman's body and not vice versa," this gown confused us totally in a play of mutual glorification of the wearer and the dress.

106 Actress Hilary Swank receiving an Oscar in 2005, wearing a Guy Laroche-designed dress that caused a stir, since her back was completely uncovered.

107 The same long dress worn by Hilary Swank, high-necked and quite chaste in front, and with long sleeves, is worn here by a model. This dress bears witness to the subtle fascination the back can exert if properly exposed by more or less plunging necklines.

Creators of Dreams

STYLISTS, TAILORS AND COUTURIERS: TRADITION AND INNOVATION

The Fascination of Haute Couture

"Fashion is foremost, an art of change," according to John Galliano. Thus stylists, while respecting the codes of etiquette that have accumulated with time, have often made the evening gown an object of experimentation. Since the early 20th century, when fashion was strongly influenced by the visual arts, the avant-garde movements and a cultural ferment in general, the desire to change, renovate, experiment with new forms and designs and to work with new materials, fabrics and decoration has been constant. This has produced results that have often been unpredictable, and creations that have not always been wearable, because, as Gianfranco Ferré stated, "Above all, never forget that fashion is also a dream."

And, perhaps, this is also the reason why some stylists have been more successful than others, imposing new rules, suggesting a new aesthetic, and lending a twist to particular moments, in the conviction that, basically, the art of tailoring is also (or above all) pure technique: knowing how to create volumes from fabric choice and cut – in other words, inventing or using small elements and details that make a difference. For example, a skirt will either fall straight or in soft folds, depending on whether or not it has been taken in; or a bodice can be made tight fitting, without special armatures, merely by adjusting the location of the stitching line. This is precisely the area in which many couturiers have worked, either respecting or overturning rules handed down through history.

Stylists like Valentino, Yves Saint Laurent, Roberto Capucci or, in more recent times, Gianni Versace and Alexander McQueen, to mention but a few, have developed the concept of fashion and experimentation, and fashion and design to become essential combinations that, very often in their work, blend to become invisible, almost non-existent. In fact, their creations take on such markedly sculptural forms that they sublimate to the utmost the concept of 'dream', of the dress that triggers one's imagination and fantasy. Whether or not it is wearable does not matter – what counts is that it be impressive and fantastical. This is achieved through the use of innovative forms, and particularly the use of new fabrics that, more often than not, are the result of scientific advances and technological innovation or experiment, for example with plissé and metal stitching. And let us not forget color and the many new and amazing shades that have helped to explore worlds formerly considered 'untouchable' and to define a new aesthetic. Black, for example, was always connected with mourning and considered attire for servants until Coco Chanel decided to use it in luxury designs made of silk, lace and light material such as chiffon, and transforming it into the evening gown color par excellence. Then there is red, a color that so stimulated the creative imagination of Valentino that he made it the distinguishing feature of his style, 'codified' in a well-defined nuance.

Therefore, this experimentation also drew inspiration from distant worlds, artistic movements, ideas that came from street life and industry; experimenting with shapes and volumes, trying to disassemble and reassemble an aesthetic that caressed the body, only to reject it immediately; and almost transforming these designs, especially evening attire, into artistic objects on which they can work and try to find new solutions, sometimes completely disregarding wearability. Since the early 1900s, the great stylists, tailors and couturiers – up to John Galliano, Vivienne Westwood, Sarah Burton and Zac Posen – have sought to revive and reinterpret the past in keeping with their own personal aesthetic vision while remaining well aware that that there is seldom anything new in the world of fashion.

Among those designers who, more than most, concentrate on making architecture and the study of forms and volumes their 'mission', the Italian stylist Roberto Capucci certainly occupies a prominent position. He is known for his commitment to experimentation with innovative fabrics which he uses to animate his creations, which are true sculptures with original, architectural forms made up of various elements – geometric, fan-shaped, cubic, ring-shaped and overlapping, as well as stylized flowers, flaming spirals, and plays of light and shade – and always with colors that enliven the fabrics. His truly artistic creations were decisive in his winning, when only 28, the Young Talent Design Award at the 1958 Boston Fashion Awards for his Box Line design, which marked a leap forward in design at the time, a sort of portent of things to come, of elements, that in following decades, would be major factors in the success of Italian fashion throughout the world in the 1980s and 1990s. Capucci was particularly fascinated by silk, which he used as a basic material that he worked and shaped and that became the distinguishing feature of his style. Being an experimenter by nature, he used a special fabric, sarsenet, a fine taffeta silk with a somewhat rigid texture that creates a faint swishing sound when the wearer moves. Considered a genius by Christian Dior, who in 1958 called him "the best creator in Italian fashion," in 1956, this stylist-sculptor designed the Nove Gonne (Nine Skirts) dress. Made of spectacular, lavish red taffeta, it consists of nine raised concentric skirts above a knee-length sheath that is shorter in front and longer, and with a train, in the back. This design became iconic in the United States, so much so that it appeared in a comic strip in the *Dallas Morning News* and was worn by Marilyn Monroe, for whom Capucci later created other designs. His gowns are timeless, with a highly recognizable style that encapsulates many other styles without appearing to do so. They are made of fabrics like taffeta and silk in bright colors juxtaposed in a unique and stunning way, all of which creates the very foundation of the gowns, highlighting their folds and structure, down to the minutest detail. And color has always remained a feature of his creations; he has experimented with color on his constructed, sculptural forms – his stylistic trademark – as well as on flowing, closer-fitting silhouettes like the white and red Peplos design created in 1973. In the late 1970s, with his column gowns, he inaugurated a series of sculptural dresses, using a great deal of plissé, which was ideal for his spectacular creations and was shaped and made even more breathtaking by those bright colors that only he was able to use and combine so masterfully. Capucci even went so far as to produce gowns that seemed to be on fire and to occupy all the space around them, creating an impressive visual effect. One of the most iconic of these was the Farfallone (Large Butterfly, 1985), made of multi-colored plissé. The Ocean model, on the other hand, again made of plissé but with various nuances of two colors, rendered the sculptural effect he always sought to achieve even more effectively. His basic idea was not to concern himself with the body-dress relationship, which does not mean sacrificing the body to his creations, but rather enhancing it until it becomes a unique work of art. In the final years of his creative activity he rejected the world of fashion, concentrating on stylistic research and experimenting with forms that were fantastic, rapturous and unusual, even for him: more than mere dresses, they have become 'sculptures to be lived in.'

113 Roberto Capucci's Nine Skirts design in red taffeta is theatrical and sumptuous.
It consists of nine overlaid concentric skirts placed over a sheath.

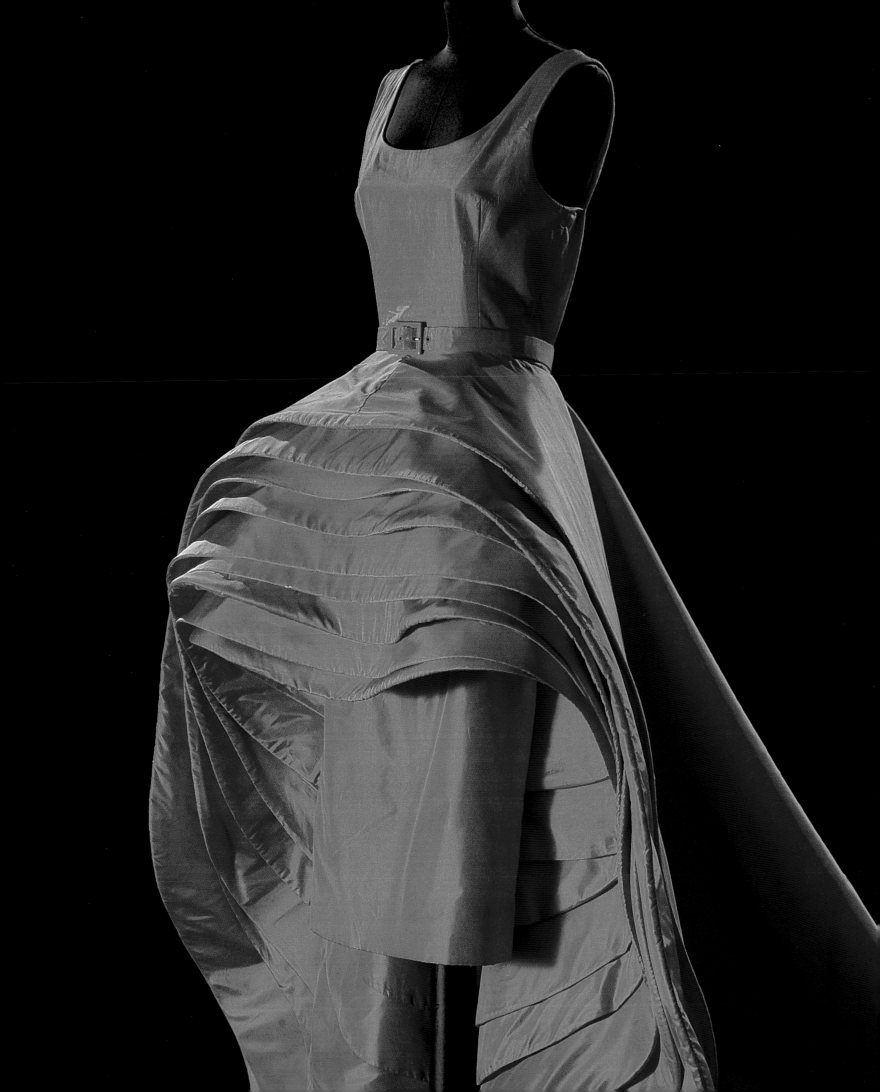

114 A sculptural dress in plissé taffeta created in 1985 in four colors, with wide, butterfly-like sleeves and an overskirt.

115 The 1985 Large Butterfly design in multicolor plissé is one of Capucci's most representative creations.

116 A large bow,
that almost becomes
a butterfly, is the
dominating motif
of this green plissé
gown.

117 The Ocean
gown, created in
1998, consists of
1200 pieces of
crinkled taffeta in 37
shades of blue.

"I know what women want. They want to be beautiful," Valentino said during an interview, and he has dedicated his entire life to this 'mission', dressing the most beautiful and most important women in the world, who reciprocated this devotion in equal measure. The first to become aware of his talent was Jackie Kennedy, who, at a dance, was awestruck by a dress that one of the other guests was wearing, which had been designed by Valentino. As a result, she purchased several of his creations, and for her wedding with Aristotle Onassis in 1968, she wore one from his Collezione Bianca or all-white collection, which raised him to the pantheon of high fashion. Nothing could come more naturally for a couturier who deeply loved women, luxury and beautiful attire, so much so that a color that characterizes many of his evening gowns, often combined with equally characteristic stylistic elements – ruche, floral elements, paillettes, plunging necklines, and flounces – became iconic and is now known as Valentino Red. He is also the stylist who, more than any other, contributed to the creation of the luxury version of hippie style: extremely elegant evening gowns adored by jet set women, with linear silhouettes embellished with feathers, flowers, fringes, beads, crystal, paillettes and very shiny fabrics. Among his most iconic creations is the one that Elizabeth Taylor wore at the premiere of *Spartacus* (1961). It was floor-length and sleeveless, with a bateau neckline and hems decorated with feathers. Another is the mint green one-shoulder gown with lace on an asymmetrical border that he created in 1967, which was worn by Jackie Kennedy during a trip to Cambodia and again in 2003 by Jennifer Lopez at the Oscars. However, certainly one of his most famous is the black and white vintage gown that Julia Roberts wore when she won the best actress Oscar for her performance in *Erin Brockovich* (2001). But how many people recall this 'detail' and the year it occurred? Valentino had designed it for his 1992 couture collection and it passed almost unnoticed. But when she wore it, almost ten years later, it immediately became part of fashion legend. A very long column dress with a train, black with a white border, it was one of Valentino's favorites, and he declared he was extremely happy to see it worn by Julia Roberts.

With time, the Valentino style, while basically remaining the same, continued to add new elements and ideas to the world of Haute Couture. For his 2002-2003 collection, he created a long red taffeta strapless gown with a siren silhouette and a light train surmounted by ample embossing. The iconic Valentino Red is accompanied by more ethereal hues such as beige, ivory, grays and almost 'powdery' pinks, which often become even more delicate and astonishing with lace and chiffon used for gowns with a soft, flowing line, revitalized by the classic decorative elements of the Valentino style, ruche and mini flounce. These elements were to be seen again in the collections of Maria Grazia Chiuri and Pierpaolo Piccioli, who became the creative directors of the Valentino fashion house in 2007 and continue in the wake of the maestro, with a linear style embellished with embroidery and quality fabrics, as well as a romantically sober allure. For that matter, Valentino once said that "Elegance is the balance between proportion, emotion and surprise."

119 The 2007-2008 fall-winter couture collection celebrated the 45th anniversary of the Valentino fashion house, presenting the main features of his style. For this pink gown Valentino used the 'organza pages' technique, with petals of fabric sewn over one another to resemble a book.

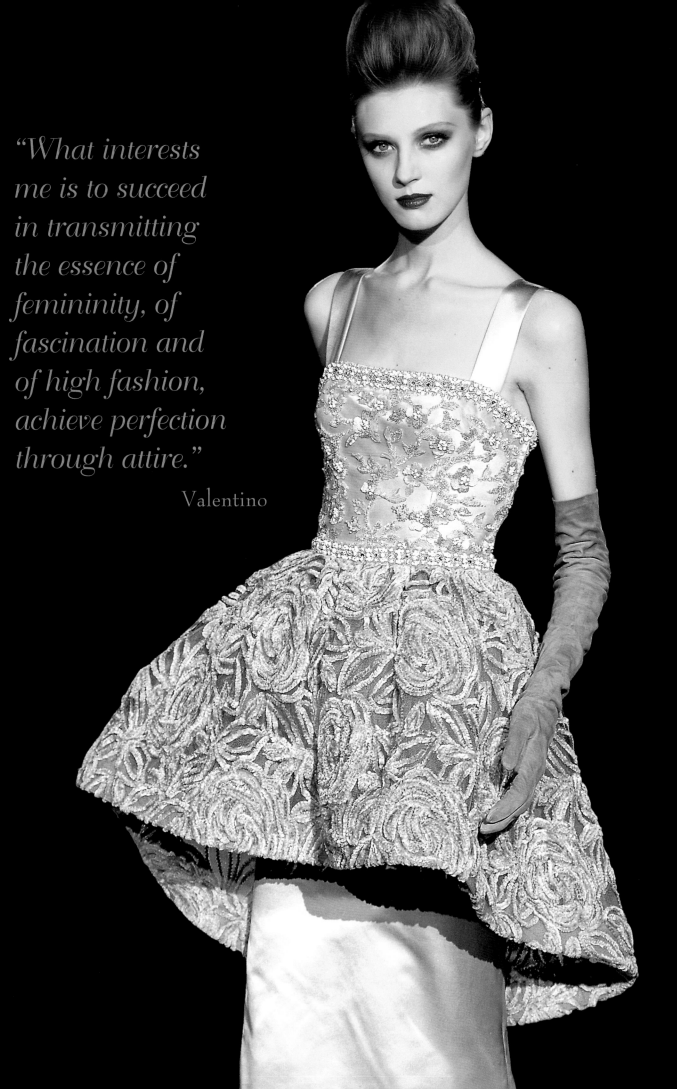

"What interests me is to succeed in transmitting the essence of femininity, of fascination and of high fashion, achieve perfection through attire."

Valentino

120 This evening gown – in satin and lace, with a pencil skirt and a stiff lampshade bodice – resembles those of the early 1900s designed by Paul Poiret. It was presented at the 2006 fall-winter couture show.

121 Fringes, beads, fine embroidery and feathers are among the decorative elements that characterize the Valentino style.

122 and 123 Red is flanked by more ethereal shades such as beige, ivory, gray and almost 'powdery' pink, often made even more astonishing thanks to the fluid fabrics with their soft, flowing line. An example is this elegant design from the 2005 spring-summer Haute Couture collection.

125 Karolina Kurkova wearing a gown in the 2005-2006 fall-winter Haute Couture collection that is embellished with a large white bow and long white gloves.

"The perfection of a dress is like a sculpture that is done on the body of a lady."

Valentino

"I know what women want.
They want to be beautiful."

Valentino

126 and 127
Valentino really loved to emphasize feminine beauty by making his designs true masterpieces of sartorial skill and decorating them with bows, flowers, fine embroidery and various types of fabric. Here are two sophisticated gowns from his 2005-2006 fall-winter Haute Couture collection.

"Innovating for Valentino [...] doesn't mean eliminating the color red, but making it in a way that resembles us, that reflects our sensitivity."

Maria Grazia Chiuri and
Pierpaolo Piccioli

128 and 129 Two gowns in the Valentino 2013 spring-summer collection designed by Maria Grazia Chiuri and Pierpaolo Piccioli, whose creations are the continuation of the master's linear style with a 'romantically sober' allure.

130 A sophisticated red is present in all Valentino collections, together with many types of fabric such as this summer 2007 design.

131 Detail of a gown in the Valentino 2013 spring-summer collection, created by Maria Grazia Chiuri and Pierpaolo Piccioli with the trademark Valentino Red.

"This was my passion:
to design dresses, I'm a
disaster in everything else!"

Valentino

Oscar de la Renta

When speaking of evening dresses one cannot ignore the sumptuous creations of Oscar de la Renta, the American stylist of Dominican origin who for about 60 years dressed the most famous and most beautiful women in the world, including many First Ladies such as Jackie Kennedy, Hillary Clinton and Nancy Reagan, a large number of actresses, Sarah Jessica Parker being one of the most enthusiastic, and Amal Alamuddin Clooney, whose magnificent wedding dress he designed. He skillfully highlighted the femininity of these famous women, always lending them a touch of timeless classical elegance, the same elegance that characterized the great 20th-century couturiers and that every woman wants to experience at least once in her lifetime. The result was obtained partly thanks to his experience working for the great fashion houses that dressed the aristocracy and upper classes during the postwar period – Balenciaga, Christian Dior, Lanvin and Balmain – where he learned the art of high fashion tailoring, which can easily be noted in the elaborate constructions of some of his designs, enlivened with decorative elements, prints and accessories that were always scintillating and betrayed their Latin provenance. One memorable creation was the one in 19th-century style worn by Sarah Jessica Parker in 2014 at the annual Met Gala, a luxurious gown with a gigantic train, a classic 'true princess' form, a black bodice with a heart-shaped neckline and white taffeta skirt. The back part reveals a puffy underskirt with a black and white print, at the lower end of which the stylist's signature stands out in red. The black and white stripes on the train had previously been used in a design presented for the stylist's 2013 spring-summer collection, on a very large train that reminded one of 18th-century panniers that have been modernized and made squarer. The 2012-2013 fall-winter collection, on the other hand, was a sort of revival of 1960s bon ton, with flowing taffeta and lace skirts in pastel colors and decorated with brooches and jewels, some of which were even printed onto the fabrics, as well as embroidery, naturally. On the other hand, for the 2012 summer collection there were very loose taffeta skirts combined with a mini lace racket. So we had the eternal uptown girl, or better, the de la Renta woman, always impeccable, who seemed to follow this master fashion designer's rule: "Walk like you have three men walking behind you."

133 A design from the 2014 spring-summer collection. The American fashion designer of Dominican origin skillfully highlighted femininity with creations that combined the essence of classical elegance with dazzling detail.

"What's most important for a woman is the projection of her individuality through fashion."

Oscar de la Renta

134 Natalia Vodianova wearing a gown designed by Oscar de la Renta for his 2002 Haute Couture collection.

135 A touch of the exotic marks this strapless columnar gown designed in 2011 that is dotted with paillettes.

"His [Oscar de la Renta's] name alone evokes elegance and timeless beauty. And his designs give each of us a chance to feel like we're special, too."

Hillary Clinton

136 This sumptuous evening dress, from 2003, harks back to 18th-century attire with its pannier skirt and bodice with a wide and low neckline.

137 A blue taffeta gown with silver embroidery, the result of a collaboration with John Galliano, for the 2013-2014 fall-winter collection.

Karl Lagerfeld

He is called the Kaiser of high fashion because of his German origins and the absolute rigor that is his distinguishing characteristic, and he designs for various fashion houses, primarily Chanel and Fendi. Lagerfeld learned his trade from two greats, Dior and Yves Saint Laurent, and, in 1965, worked for the Fendi sisters, designing their fur line. And he did so with an irreverent, non-conformist spirit, coloring the furs and cutting them in unusual ways to create the Fun Fur phenomenon (hence the iconic logo of the fashion house, FF). Success came in 1983 when he became the creative director of Chanel, which was on the brink of collapse. But Kaiser Karl succeeded in reviving the label and making it a cult throughout the world. "Its style is that of another epoch, but it has resisted and has adapted to the modernity of the following decades." This is Chanel according to Karl Lagerfeld, whose ideal of femininity has always been the model Inès de la Fressange, certainly not romantic or precious, just as Coco Chanel herself never was. Therefore, the style, as designed by Lagerfeld, is suitable for all women of whatever age and is presented in fashion shows that have become spectacles. "Chanel elegance is an attitude, a spirit, a form of rejection of femininity full of frills." Attire of a timeless elegance that is still subject to experimentation and changes, but always respecting the original style created by Mademoiselle Coco, as can be seen in the details, the decorative elements, and in the forms that, almost always starting off from linear silhouettes, play with volumes without radically altering the lines of the body. In the 2013-2014 fall-winter collection the bon ton was 'mitigated' by a sort of rock allure while remaining chic. This was obtained through the use of black, lace, see-through and leather details. The colors were equally sober, from neutral whites and greys to beiges, blues and blacks. At times, there appeared the bright hues of pink, light blue, orange, gold and fuchsia, as in the 2014-2015 fall-winter collection and, above all, in the 2015 spring-summer collection – a virtual garden in which the gowns became so many multicolor flowers. "When you buy a Chanel product you buy an idea, more or less unconscious, depending on the knowledge one has concerning this story. The Chanel style is an idea, but it is an idea carved in a sort of collective memory, and this is something rather rare. It is a visualizable legend, a cosmopolitan phenomenon." This is how Karl Lagerfeld described the 'phenomenon' that is Chanel.

139 Karl Lagerfeld, creative director of the Chanel fashion house since 1983, favors elegant, but not precious, femininity. Here, in July 1992, Claudia Schiffer is wearing a theatrical headdress.

"*The Chanel style is that of another epoch, but it has resisted and has adapted to the modernity of the following decades.*"

Karl Lagerfeld

140 Black feathers and small studs decorate the back part and the hem of a gown from the 2004-2005 fall-winter Haute Couture collection.

141 Details and precious decorative elements reveal the essence of the Chanel couture style. The paillette and crystal decoration on this dress, in the 2006-2007 fall-winter collection, is also seen on the shoes.

142 In his 2014 spring-summer collection, Karl Lagerfeld succeeded in imparting sporty chic allure to Haute Couture, creating elegant designs that reveal fine sartorial skill and have brilliant details. Here is a design with an American neckline.

143 Another gown in the same collection, this time made of black tulle enlivened with feathers. The ultra-chic appeal is tempered and made sporty by the sneakers.

"I like the idea of adopting materials that are not usually used in Haute Couture."

Karl Lagerfeld

144 With Kaiser Karl, it begins with a linear silhouette and then he works on the volumes, inventing new forms that set off the lines of the body.

145 Karl Lagerfeld introduced new materials to the runway, for example neoprene combined with tulle, chiffon, lace and organza.

Giorgio Armani

Armani – the name says it all. He is the very essence of chic, with a purity of line that is synonymous with a femininity that draws from masculinity while never forgetting its female quality. Beauty with a capital B expressed through forms that are always suggestive rather than specific, accompanied by powder-like colors ranging from beige to blue, and up to 'greige', a combination of grey and beige, a hue that has become a trademark, a characteristic feature of Armani's style. In the 1990s, his women became more sensual and feminine, with evening gowns that retained his style in sober, clean forms but were embellished with decorative elements such as his satin kimonos and shantung, which testify to his interest in the Orient, especially Japan. In 2005, Giorgio Armani launched an Haute Couture line, Giorgio Armani Privé, whose aesthetic respects the essence of his style with simple designs formed by strong exotic Oriental and Middle Eastern influences. The blue turbans, typical of the Tuareg, enhance the satin and silk evening gowns presented in his 2011 spring-summer collection, with their tapering lines embellished with jets and paillettes, all dominated by blue, an iconic Armani color on the same level as beige and grey. And the 2014 Giorgio Armani Privé spring-summer collection was dedicated to elements taken from tribal nomadic costumes, such as tulle and organza, which made for light gowns with skin-tight bodices and skirts that are slightly wider at the waist, adorned with crystals and gemstones. For his 2014-2015 winter collection, he used three colors – white, black and red – the last of which was used for a gown with a siren silhouette and a bodice that became a kind of cocoon, in which the bust almost seemed to want to hide. "Even if she is young, a woman who chooses couture wants to be beautiful, unique, precious and not anachronistic," Armani said, condensing his idea of Haute Couture. And he added that "Haute couture allows me to be different from myself." This year marks the 10th birthday of the Privé line, celebrated with a collection whose bamboo leitmotif with its strength, delicacy and gracefulness, are a perfect combination to represent women who are equally strong and delicate. "I have tried to describe this oxymoron with a high fashion collection. This is my tribute to style and beauty for a new generation. A proud and soft woman, like bamboo," the great stylist declared at the end of the show.

147 Giorgio Armani's 2015 spring-summer Privé collection revolves around bamboo, a metaphor for strength and delicacy that is printed on this long China blue gown, which is an ideal representation of a proud woman.

148 and 149 In the 2008 spring-summer Privé collection Giorgio Armani concentrated more on forms than on colors, lending greater movement to his designs through structures created with ruche, flounces, spirals and fan shapes in light, lucid or transparent fabrics.

150 and 151 A 'lunar woman,' dressed in a long siren gown made of glittering fabric on the catwalk at the presentation of Giorgio Armani's 2011 spring-summer Privé collection, which was inspired by precious stones such as rubies, sapphires, emeralds and diamonds.

152 At his 2014-15 fall-winter Privé collection, featuring designs in reds and blacks, Giorgio Armani stated that it was time to go back to making women dream. Here, clouds of organza lend vitality to a design that becomes a fiery red tangle.

153 Giorgio Armani's 2014 spring-summer Privé collection was dedicated to nomadic women who wore light tulle and organza designs with tight-fitting bodices embroidered with crystal and stones, and skirts that puff out slightly at the waist.

154 and 155 These gowns with a bustier and a rather wide skirt and animated by mini-flounces are enclosed by tulle veils decorated with red dots and Swarovski stones.

A pupil of Christian Dior, and heir to his fashion house, Yves Saint Laurent gave women the first glimpses of modernity, especially as regards Haute Couture, which he upgraded with numerous innovations and a unique, forward-looking style with many influences and references drawn from different worlds: the streets, the exoticism of distant lands, art, cinema, and music. "I participated in the transformation of my era. I did it with clothes, which are surely less important than music, architecture, painting… but for whatever it's worth, I did it," he said. From the outset, he demonstrated his great originality, inventing, in 1958, a new line, the so-called trapeze dress, which he included in a collection that to some extent evoked certain iconic elements of Dior, such as the fabrics he used and the smart embellishments, combined with softer, innovative elements such as less rounded, trape-zoidal shoulders. This marked the end of the Maison Dior's elaborate creations and the beginning of lighter and straighter lines that were more comfortable to wear. And practicality was Saint Laurent's innovation because he immediately understood that new social customs called for a faster rhythm and required more dynamic and less elaborate creations. As far as evening gowns were concerned, this spurred on the drive for new solutions, above all the Tuxedo Dress, the transparent creations, and the boho-chic style with its many exotic influences taken from the traditional dress of countries like Russia and China. Saint Laurent dedicated two collections to these designs: long, pleated skirts, short hussar jackets, fur coats and brocade – all characterized by bright colors, the juxtaposition of rich and different fabrics, prints and exotic decorative elements. The 1967 Bambara collection, on the other hand, was inspired by Africa and featured beads, raffia, vivacious colors and shells.

YSL's love of all things feminine, and some of his close friendships with women were fundamental to the evolution of his style: Loulou de la Falaise, a dear friend and muse, inspired him with her chic original style, which he translated into gypsy-inspired designs. "Over the years I have learned that what is important in a dress is the woman who is wearing it," he stated. And this conviction may have influenced the creation of one his most iconic designs, in early 1966, the Tuxedo Dress, the famous evening wear for men transformed for women, a major contribution to the evolution of the evening gown that marked a 'subversive' departure from the past. And this was repeated in 1968, when he presented one of the most iconic evening gowns of all time, in totally transparent chiffon with ostrich feathers on the hips, the precursor of the nude look. One of his favorite and oft-repeated statements was "There's not one black, but many blacks." As an absolute master of color, he created juxtapositions no one else had ever dared to attempt: fuchsia rose and orange, brown and black, and especially black and blue – the fruit of his great love of art and a tribute to the great 20th-century artists and avant-garde movements. "Fashion is not art, but to make clothes one must be an artist," he once stated. And, in a highly personal way, he contributed to art by printing innovative creations on fabrics that spurred on the 'modernization' of Haute Couture. For example, he is to be credited with having invented color blocking, the combination of blocks of bold colors that are contrasting but in the end form a harmonious and vibrant whole, as can easily be seen in certain of his designs that have become icons of high fashion.

157 Yasmeen Ghauri wearing a silk gown with black and white stripes and a matching stole from the 1992 spring-summer Haute Couture collection.

One example of this is the ankle-length evening gown from his 1966 Pop Art collection, a tribute to the burgeoning artistic movement and to one of its most representative exponents, Tom Wesselmann: linear form, a dark blue and pink silhouette motif of a woman printed on the left side of the dress. Later on, especially in the 1970s and 1980s, he was influenced by great painters such as Picasso, Braque and Matisse, as well as by the almost violent colors of Fauvism. He revered these artists and had the following to say about his relationship with them: "My aim was not to challenge the great masters, but to approach them in order to learn as much as possible from their genius." 1980 witnessed a collection dedicated to Matisse and the Fauves, featuring designs with a tight bodice and skirts that took on volume around the waist, becoming a sort of canvas on which Yves Saint Laurent offered his personal vision of the artist's oeuvre and the artistic movement, with prints and patches of color that portrayed and celebrated its visual essence. In 1988, it was Picasso's turn, with a collection entirely dedicated to the great Spanish artist and the Cubist movement, dominated by almost sculptural, highly colorful jackets and by special forms placed on linear black skirts. In 2002 Saint Laurent retired from the world of fashion and the catwalks, celebrated by a show and by a phrase that epitomizes not only the essence of his work but of his 'duty,' his 'mission': "I always wanted to put myself at the service of women. I wanted to accompany them in the great movement for liberation that occurred in the last century."

158 A luxurious velvet gown with a bateau neckline. Long sleeves and white organza ruche decorate the ample A-line skirt.

159 Very few couturiers were able to enhance femininity like Yves Saint Laurent. He was one of the first to use see-through in high fashion. Here, Naomi Campbell is seen wearing a sexy design with a black lace bodice that was part of the stylist's 2000-2001 fall-winter collection.

"Fashion is not art, but to make clothes one must be an artist."

Yves Saint Laurent

160 January 2002: Yves Saint Laurent's farewell to Haute Couture at the famous show celebrating his brilliant career, with 105 models presenting
300 of his most iconic creations. Here, Katoucha Niane is wearing a cloak from his 1988 collection, which drew inspiration from Cubism.

161 The great stylist loved art and was influenced by Matisse, Picasso, Warhol and Braque, among others. An example of this is his
La Guitare, one of the designs in his 1988 Cubist-inspired collection, worn by Katoucha Niane during his 2002 farewell show.

Vivienne Westwood

Vivienne Westwood is considered the 'queen of punk,' the movement for which she, together with her first husband Malcolm McLaren, helped to create an aesthetic in the late 1970s that is still much alive and highly recognizable, and at the time was provocative and revolutionary. Non-conformism and respect for tradition are the two watchwords of her style, which are seemingly antithetical but are perfectly compatible in her hands. A visionary, eccentric and surreal – like the British stylists in the 1980s and 1990s, of whom she was the leader and pioneer – Westwood has constantly drawn inspiration from tradition and history, which she has analyzed in all epochs and reproduced in evening dresses with theatrical and lavish designs often made of British fabrics like tweed and tartan: from extremely tight corsets to ample crinolines and skirt-panniers, perfect for modern metropolitan female 'courtiers'. The Watteau Dress, shown at her 1996 spring-summer collection, is memorable: emerald green, made of silk, taffeta and chamois leather, this gown was inspired by the attire in the canvases of the great 18th-century French painter and presented in grand style by model Linda Evangelista. Westwood's 2003 Anglophilia fall-winter collection was the perfect synthesis of her aesthetic, with lines that referred to the past, and fabrics such as tartan. Her street style is always well represented in her collections, which are often so lavish that the shows become spectacles that, in some cases, are transformed into passionate forms of social protest. The 2010 Gaia collection was a tribute to Mother Earth, featuring asymmetrical forms, drapery skillfully placed on the silhouette, and prints referencing nature. Two years later, at the end of the 2011-2012 fall-winter Gold Label show, the stylist stated: "I can't continue the battle over climate change, so I've decided to express my thoughts concerning our planet and climate change through strong women, because, in fact, women are the guardians of culture." And so she did, with designs that drew inspiration from various places in the world, including *animalier* and batik prints, floral motifs and Scottish tartan, all used on forms that combine strength and romanticism, with wide skirts and puff sleeves.

163 In her 2015 spring-summer collection the transgressive, rebellious Vivienne Westwood battles against the destruction of our earth, creating puffy forms influenced by 18th-century fashion and enhancing her designs with nature-inspired patterns.

164 This stunning bronze gown in Westwood's 2005-2006 fall-winter Gold Label collection harks back to 19th-century crinoline.

165 The back of this silk taffeta design has sophisticated drapery that highlights the bateau neck bodice with striking, iridescent bronze.

166-167 The 2015-2016 fall-winter collection is a protest against pollution, climate change and British politics in general. Here, we see an extremely voluminous evening dress with grunge influences.

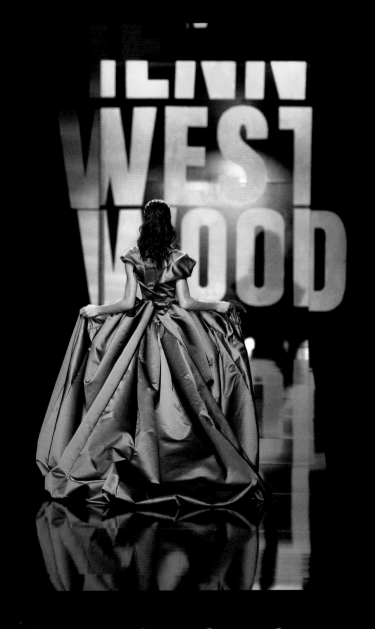

"*I take something from the past which has a sort of vitality that has never been exploited – like crinoline – and I reinterpret it. In the end you have got something original because you have added your idea.*"

Vivienne Westwood

"I can't continue
the battle over
climate change,
so I've decided
to express my
thoughts
concerning
our planet and
climate change
through strong
women, because,
in fact, women
are the guardians
of culture."

Vivienne Westwood

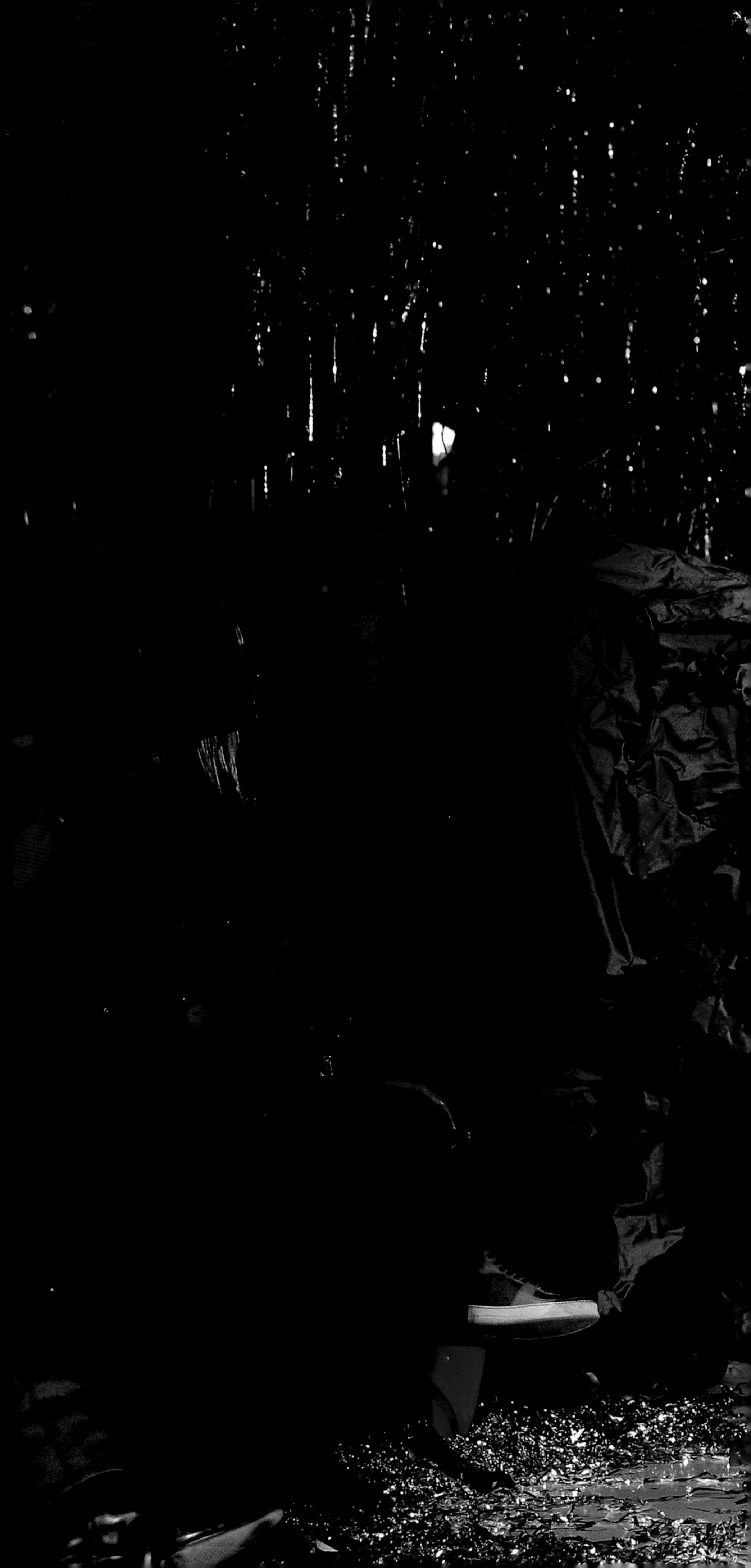

The 'architect of fashion' and one of the couturiers who made Italian fashion so great and who always paid particular attention to the fields of design and art, liked to repeat a quotation by another architect, Mies van der Rohe, that for the most part encapsulates his own aesthetic: "We keep our feet firmly on the ground but reach for the stars with our head." This was precisely what Gianfranco Ferré searched for with his style, clothing that would be a synthesis of great sartorial skill and an innovative use of materials, such as silk, chiffon and taffeta in original combinations that drew inspiration from his many trips to the Orient, especially India, a country he dearly loved and that would influence his perception of color and form. In his hands, these were in perfect symbiosis, in a mutually advantageous relationship. He often used colors in bright and dazzling juxtapositions to heighten the shape of his dresses, as only Roberto Capucci had succeeded in doing before him: reds typical of Chinese lacquer, gold and orange of Indian saris, blues and greens. "Even when it is luxurious and has a sartorial slant, ready-to-wear is always ready-to-wear, therefore more generic and indistinctive. By contrast, high fashion responds solely to particular needs, to the specific interests of the women for whom it is designed," Ferré used to say. And his evening gowns are unique masterpieces, made with fabrics that are never ordinary and are perfectly adapted for the creation of his architectural forms. "No georgette, no sense of softness. Rather, full textures adapting easily to the volumes suggested by the cut. Shiny wool/cotton. Matte gazars. Gorgeous silk shantung, duchesse, faille, double-face taffeta/wool. Picqué heightening the tridimensional feel of particular working processes. Airy fabrics adding a sheer quality to turquoise, a dazzling brilliance to red," he said when discussing his 1988 spring-summer High Fashion collection. Gianfranco Ferré, who, in 1989, became artistic director of the Maison Dior, was also the stylist who persuaded women to wear white shirts as elegant evening dress. "In the lexicon of contemporary elegance, I like to think that the white shirt is a universal term that each woman may 'pronounce' as she prefers." Elevated to the rank of evening dress and iconic garment, it became what some have defined as "the paradigm of the Ferré style," always presented in his collections like a subtle leitmotif that, for every occasion, takes on different details, volumes, materials and forms. He called the white shirt "the mark of my style," a spur to redefine codes of elegance in the 1980s, epitomizing its most discreet aspect, which is no less sensual. Among his iconic designs is Chalice, presented in the 1982 fall-winter collection, made of gazar that somewhat resembles an arum lily, with a bustier around the waist and two strips of fabric that cover the front part of the bust. Finally, the Origami shirt is the sublimation of Ferré's background: created, for the 2004 spring-summer collection, in pleated tulle, it departed from traditional canons and became a true sculpture piece that referred to Japanese origami. When Ferré died, in 2007, the fashion house was entrusted to the stylists Aquilano.Rimondi, who are continuing to design in the master's sartorial tradition, with structured and architectural forms marked by their sober and sophisticated elegance.

169 The jewels in Ferré's 2006 spring-summer collection were dedicated to the Virgin of Guadalupe.

"White is not only a color; it is a declaration of vitality and purity."

Gianfranco Ferré

170 The 2006 spring-summer collection featured the fascination of Latin women. The linear georgette dress is dazzling thanks to exquisite embroidery and crystals.

171 White, representing vitality and purity, was chosen to highlight forms and volumes, as in this bustier that adheres to the hips and the skirt that descends in an A-line.

172 With his 2006-2007 fall-winter collection, the stylist sought to accentuate, even more, the purity of the form, imparting the idea of regality that is both severe and graceful, as in this sensual yet austere black gown that exposes the shoulders and most of the back.

173 Two gowns from the same collection that clearly reveal Ferré's aim to lend a touch of 'rational' opulence to the ideal of pure form through the magic of light and measured decorative elements.

The stylist who is the emblem of the hedonism and joie de vivre of the 1980s, is remembered for the glam he surrounded himself with; for the strong and incisive image of women and femininity that he created; for the group of top models that he helped to become living legends; for the Medusa, the symbol of his fashion house; for the gold that was the dominating color of his stylistic universe; and for the celebrities who adored him and, with him, formed a true court, a kind of mutual benefit society: the friendship with rock stars and actors increased his fame through their very presence, and he in turn designed their clothes, taking them into an almost other-worldly dimension.

But Gianni Versace was also a tireless experimenter with materials and forms, an inventor of styles and details that marked a milestone in the history of fashion and its mores, as well as a formidable creator of an aesthetic that pervaded an entire decade. He created audacious femininity by using traditional elements, reinterpreting them and proposing attire based on exhibiting the body with clinging, asymmetrical lines that left most of it exposed. He referenced the past. For example, his 'siren' gowns evoked those designed by Madeleine Vionnet, which he combined with punk culture by using safety pins that held the various parts together. Or he would use color as only Sonia Delaunay was able to create (and in 1990 he dedicated a gown to her, which he called Dress for Sonia Delaunay), with a palette of dazzling hues. On the other hand, the fuchsia and green Torchon design created in 1986 is sculptural. And, just as he used color, he worked with prints, with the same aesthetic sensitivity as Andy Warhol's, to whom he paid tribute in 1991 with an ankle-length, tight fitting evening gown dedicated to Pop Art that had the faces of Marilyn Monroe and James Dean printed on the fabric.

Versace had a very close relationship with art and art history, which influenced many of his creations. "Fashion is Art and Art collaborates with Fashion," he liked to say. He drew inspiration from classical art for some of his most alluring evening dresses. These were both long and short peplos gowns with folds and slits, and necklines held up by shoulder straps embellished with medals with the famous Versace logo of the Medusa. They were made of fine-textured fabrics, as shiny as satin, creating an effect suggestive of the smooth white surface of ancient statues or with loose folds and plissé to refer to the typical fluting of Doric columns. And it was with fabric, and slits, that Gianni Versace loved to experiment: sculpted leather, vinyl and jersey, often combined, and Oroton, the metal mesh fabric that he himself invented. In 1982, he introduced the Oroton tunic dress, which he included in all of his later collections, together with gowns with disparate forms, long and tapering with low necklines revealing cleavage or with bateau necklines and wide slits in gold, silver and bronze. His final collection, in fall-winter 1997-1998, marked another step forward, because the Oroton dresses were now decorated with Byzantine crosses, embroidery and applied beadwork. With him, the corset became an evening gown, graced by slits and cuts and by materials like pvc and vinyl in order to impart a futuristic allure.

1992 marked one of Versace's most famous and emblematic collections, Bondage, featuring fig-ure-hugging black gowns decorated with gilded studs, buckles and diamonds. This showed us that Italy's most revolutionary fashion designer never limited himself to a single source of inspiration; in fact, his collections revealed the different influences made by art, rock music and street life.

So, Maison Versace, the emblem of sensuality, is still very much alive. The stylist's sister, Donatella, became its chief designer after Gianni's death in 1997 and, like her brother, she counts many rock stars, models and actresses in her entourage. Donatella modernized the image of the Versace woman, main-taining her sex appeal and glamor while adding a touch of power and determination: the Versace siren has become somewhat of a bad girl as well. These new elements now characterize the high fashion Versace Atelier line, featuring extremely elegant creations with skin-tight, siren-like lines decorated with the typical Versace materials: the metal mesh fabric, vivacious colors and fine embroidery, sexy slits and corsets that reveal inches of naked flesh – all of which is a tribute to a femininity that combines sensuality and glamor, the epitome of the Versace brand.

176 This long, black silk dress is influenced by Madeleine Vionnet's siren dresses, cut diagonally and 'contaminated' with punk elements that, however, are no longer safety pins, but buckles.

177 The bodice of this aquamarine gown in the Versace 2009 spring-summer collection suggests an architectural structure; it is tight around the midriff, thus highlighting the shoulders, while the skirt flows down the legs with an opening in front.

178 Versace epitomized audacious femininity with creations that adapt perfectly to the body, leaving a lot of it exposed. The 2015 Atelier spring-summer collection renovates this spirit with gowns that enhance the silhouette with strategically placed cuts and slits.

179 This black silk cady evening dress in the same collection highlights the sensuality of the arms and shoulders using gossamer and crystal.

film *Yesterday, Today and Tomorrow* (1963) with her wardrobe of slips, corsets and lace. In the mid-1980s, a period dominated by Giorgio Armani's minimalism and Gianni Versace's Pop sensuality, the fashion duo Dolce & Gabbana proposed femininity with a wholly Mediterranean retro flavor, reviving and reinterpreting codes of Italian tradition, especially from Sicily – its age-old customs, iconic images, colors, and even its scents and flavors – all incorporated and transformed into that subtle leitmotif that would become their aesthetic. Thus, their ideal woman was mysterious, a seductress, but not impertinent; and this was achieved especially with the bustier, which became their iconic trademark par excellence, together with lace and leopard-skin prints, as part of their representative slip dresses or an accessory reinterpreted in many different ways. Already in 1991 the singer and songwriter Madonna flaunted one of these bustiers, encrusted with colored crystals and charms, at the premiere of *Truth or Dare* (1991) accompanied by a black coat and a pair of cuissards. In 1995, the duo proposed the same article in a 'soft' sado-masochistic version, with see-through and a slightly tightened waist, worn on the runway by a splendid Carla Bruni holding a riding crop. 2007 featured a tribute to Thierry Mugler, with a dress-bustier in metal producing an armature effect that was later worn by Lady Gaga for the launch of her album *Paparazzi*, and other designs that resembled modern armatures that were long, close fitting and with very tight belts and silvered fabrics. Black lace and white taffeta were the protagonists of the 2009 collection, while the 2012-2013 fall-winter collection, inspired by Luchino Visconti's artistic universe and his famous movie *The Leopard* (1963) featured dresses with a bustier and a short pannier skirt, in a blaze of black and golden lace. Black see-through and colored stones on a bustier were presented at the following, 2013, spring-summer collection.

Dolce & Gabbana's evening dresses, corolla-shaped designs with a narrow waist and flaring skirts, are also influenced by the past. And, while the forms may be classical, these stylists like to experiment with details and fabrics. For example, the 2013 spring-summer collection features wicker baskets and skirts and bustiers with an armature of interwoven rush, covered with tulle or transparent black muslin, and with a bra and black culottes underneath. There are also more romantic and flowing designs, such as those featured in the 2011-2012 fall-winter collection, which are very loose and rustling, either black or in pastel colors like turquoise and old rose. Their first Haute Couture collection was presented in 2012, obviously in Sicily, in Taormina, and included all the touchstone components of their style. The show was almost an apotheosis of Italian sartorial tradition inspired once again, needless to say, by the movie *The Leopard* in a super luxury version: attire that referred to 19th-century crinoline, embroidered and richly decorated with hand-painting, made of lace, taffeta and brocade as well as black sheaths made of skin-tight lace and transparent so that the undergarments were clearly visible. These same elements were presented in subsequent collections: in 2013, with skirts with prints of some of the most famous monuments in Italy, and up to the 2014-2015 fall-winter designs, which seemed to have arrived directly from the 19th-century atelier of Mr. Worth and the Victorian Age, while the prints and decorative elements referred to Capri, with its typical colors and majolica. "Every piece must be unique. It is not only choosing a dress; it is a bit like selecting a work of art," the duo stated when discussing their high fashion line.

181 Sicily is the leitmotif of Dolce & Gabbana style, always featured in every collection and a fertile source of inspiration. Examples of this are the baroque lace dresses presented on the runway of the 2012-2013 fall-winter fashion show.

182 In the 2006 spring-summer collection, the runway was transformed into a hay barn and featured creations inspired by 19th-century crinoline designs with black taffeta skirts and organza overskirts with floral motifs.

183 Natasha Poly wearing a spectacular green and white evening gown with floral motifs.

84 and 184-185 Inspired by the exquisite Byzantine mosaics in the Cathedral of Monreale and by St. Agatha, the patron saint of Catania, the 2013-2014 fall-winter collection is an explosion of color: from gold to the glittering red that prevailed in the grand finale featuring mini-dresses and slip dresses made of lace.

186 and 187 The opulence of the decorative elements is both tempered and sustained by the light silhouettes, which leave room for embroidery, prints and worked stones, transforming

The 2015 spring-summer collection was dedicated to 17th-century Seville and the influence Spain had on Sicily. The Sacred Heart, reproduced on the dresses and bodices, was the main element and was on all the designs presented at the show.

The decoration on this matador-style bolero jacket consists of metal, heart-shaped ex-votos, surrounded by embroidery and stones that represent flames, the symbol of everlasting love.

190 Spanish tradition was also evoked in the high-necked, three-quarter sleeve, black lace gowns with a tantalizing and subtle use of see-through, offering glimpses of the culotte and the bra.

191 Detail of a net dress with passementerie decoration.

"*Think only of how a woman feels wearing a dress that fits like a glove. She is so much at her ease that her entire personality emerges.*"

Domenico Dolce and Stefano Gabbana

"Fashion is foremost an art of change," according to John Galliano, the stylist who has made meta-morphosis his trademark and lifestyle, always a step ahead of others and never conventional. Even when he designed for other fashion houses – Givenchy in 1995 and Christian Dior the following year, two pillars of Haute Couture – he was able to assimilate and reinterpret this imposing legacy in an original manner, totally respecting the distinguishing features of his illustrious predecessors with the intelligence of those who know how to revive the past and adapt it to the contemporary scene. For Givenchy Haute Couture, he 'designed' a woman who was both seductive and ethereal, with gowns that resembled lingerie in semi-transparent fabrics, heightened by slits, low necklines, ruche and volants. When he became creative director of Maison Dior in 1996, Galliano again presented the standards and style of elegance that had so distinguished Christian Dior and, to a certain degree, always recurred in the great couturier's work of the 1940s and 1950s. The 2008-2009 fall-winter Haute Couture collection was an explicit tribute to the New Look, while the 2005-2006 fall-winter collection was a mixture and comparison of different styles, in a blaze of necklines, volumes and see-through.

Remaining intact are the dreams, romanticism and the concept of elegance of former times that spring from his masterful tailoring skills, the distinguishing feature of this English stylist, the first person from his country to head a prestigious French fashion house. His collections are filled with details referencing the past, details that re-emerge through an aesthetic whose strong point is its theatrical character, with ample, voluminous gowns, brilliant colors and accessories that often steal the show. They can be ball gowns in the pure Charles Worth style or dresses that evoke the thin silhouettes of designs by René Gruau, which Galliano revived in the 2011 Christian Dior spring-summer Haute Couture collection, another explicit tribute, this time to the post-war years, with luxurious gowns with ample skirts consisting of layers of tulle and taffeta, topped by bodices that were either rigid or more linear and close fitting, accompanied by small hats and veils. "Simplicity is such a bore! Sometimes the real fun is in bad taste!" he once said, a statement that wholly represents the essence of his style. 2003 marked the birth of his prêt-à-porter line, with a style that maintained his usual expressive power and theatrical pizzazz. This continued until 2011, when he was suspended by Maison Dior, and the fashion world, after a controversial and regrettable episode. This was followed by collections presented in his name but without his being present: the 2012 spring-summer 'Galliano without Galliano' show, officially created by his assistant Bill Gaytten and featuring siren style attire, close fitting with plenty of see-through and 'now-you-see-it-now-you-don't' effects inspired by actresses in black-and-white movies, but without their romantic allure. John Galliano's most recent appearance was in 2015, when he made his debut at the Maison Margiela with the Artisanal collection, which was marked by its pure creativity with diversified influences and above all by the felicitous compromise between the trademark Galliano theatricality and Margiela minimalism. Anna Wintour said, "Many of John's typical elements that we know and love are there, but he has possessed the Margiela vocabulary and translated it in an innovative and fascinating way."

193 Galliano's 2004-2005 fall-winter collection is a mix and match of different styles and influences produced by reinterpreting the past through contemporary details.

194 John Galliano's dresses can only be described as spectacular and eye-catching, often due to their dazzling colors and accessories. Here is a design from his 2004-2005 fall-winter collection.

195 Despite their lavish and seemingly excessive forms and decorative elements, Galliano's creations highlight strong and seductive femininity. In this design, the narrow waist is set off by the corset and voluminous pannier.

96 The gowns Galliano designed for the 2011 Christian Dior spring-summer Haute Couture collection reference the timeless elegance of the 1950s and remind one of the thin figures in René Gruau's illustrations.

97 The 'protagonist' of this design is the tulle, which is doubled over the rigid silk bodice, decorated with buttons and sprigs of flowers.

198 A dress from the 2011 spring-summer collection, which set out to express the glamor of Maison Dior through the illustrations of Gruau, who helped create the image of this fashion house in the postwar period.

199 The opulence of the forms is tempered by pastel colors.

200 Luxurious ball gowns with billowing skirts made up of layers of tulle, taffeta, chiffon, rigid or tight-fitting bodices, accompanied by small hats and veils, are the essence of the 2011 Couture spring-summer collection.

201 This lavish pearl-grey silk gown is embellished with overlaid flounces that cross the bustier and descend along the side of the overskirt.

Elie Saab

The interpreter of that timeless elegance that feeds on classical elements, beginning with such refined fabrics as silk, lace, chiffon either embroidered or covered with light crystal and bead decoration – this is the Lebanese stylist Elie Saab. He is a favorite among high society women, both royalty and celebrities, generating in his designs the most romantic allure while at the same time underscoring their most feminine and coquettish side with see-through and veiled sections, which prompted him to state: "If a woman doesn't look for luxury she will never be elegant."

A tailor more than a stylist, Elie Saab resembles the great couturiers of the past – for example Dior, Balenciaga, or Balmain – who loved the female body and enhanced it with the passion of those who never do anything at random and know that only a well-located stitch or a well-calculated play of 'now-you-see-now-you-don't' can make all the difference. In fact, in 2002, the gown Saab designed for Halle Berry, who won an Oscar as best leading actress for her performance in *Monster's Ball* (2001), immediately established him as a protagonist of high fashion. This was a beautiful gown that Berry wore with the utmost elegance and naturalness: a sheer net top with masterfully crafted embroidery in the right places, and a burgundy-colored, tight-fitting satin skirt with a very long and full train. This was the first time a Middle Eastern stylist had designed a gown for an actress at the Academy Awards ceremony, and it was to happen again with Halle Berry the following year and up to the 2014 Oscars, when a marvelous beige siren gown with crystals was worn by Angelina Jolie – a sophisticated, luxuriant and romantic design that epitomized Elie Saab's style.

His runway debut was in 2000, when his stylistic features were already well defined: sinuous lines, either figure-hugging or ball gowns that are tight around the waist then open out into volumes that are never excessive and always strategically calibrated. In fact, sobriety and precision are the watchwords of his style, which is based on delicate nuances of pastel hues. Yet these may suddenly become striking reds or burgundies, as in his 2013-2014 Haute Couture fall-winter collection, or the blues, yellows, purples and greens in the 2008 spring-summer fashion show. These two collections were less ethereal than others, in which the lines seemed to cling more to the body, delicately accompanying its movement, while still emphasizing the sexy aspect of every woman through necklines and refined see-through.

203 Embroidery, see-through and floral lace appliqué constitute the essence of the style of one of the couturiers who has made classical elegance his trademark. This photograph shows a detail from a gown in the Couture spring-summer 2014 line.

"*Every woman wants to feel beautiful. There is no longer a specific identity in fashion; they all speak the same language and want to be elegant.*"

Elie Saab

204 and 205 The Lebanese stylist creates a sense of fascination and mystery by emphasizing the coquettish side of femininity with see-through and veil, as in these two gowns from his 2012-2013 fall-winter couture collection worn by Karlie Kloss.

*"If a woman doesn't look for luxury
she will never be elegant."*

Elie Saab

206 and 207 Saab's 2014 spring-summer couture collection drew inspiration from Lawrence Alma-Tadema's paintings
and included gowns – made of silk faille and chiffon dotted with embroidery and crystals – that start off with a slim waistline,
which then opens out into a full skirt with more sinuous lines.

*"The silhouette is fundamental,
it adds femininity and sensuality.
It is the form that makes you sexy,
then comes the embroidery."*

Elie Saab

210-211 and 211 Saab's style is based on delicate nuances of pastel colors that may explode in bright shades like the red, blue and gold that characterized his 2014-2015 fall-winter couture collection.

Alexander McQueen

An Englishman who was an eccentric visionary like his fellow countryman John Galliano, whom he replaced as creative director of Maison Givenchy from 1997 to 2001, Alexander McQueen was known for his imaginative and spectacular style, which was certainly visionary and permeated with Gothic influences, with animal-like details heightened by metal decorative elements and materials like lace, which, instead of tempering the almost sado-masochistic features of some of his creations, actually served to highlight them. Known as the 'hooligan of Haute Couture' for the capacity and inclination to subvert the rules of high fashion, like Galliano he was gifted with exceptional sartorial skill, the result of his experience and work with tailors in Savile Row, know-how that he used in his near-architectural constructions more to create their precision rather than to highlight their spectacular quality. And his fashion shows were certainly spectacular, partly thanks to the fact that the models had to struggle mightily to maintain their balance while wearing preposterous, surreal high shoes (the now-iconic Armadillo Shoes, which appeared in the 2010 spring-summer collection) and dress-sculptures that often challenged the force of gravity, covered with metal scales, fresh flowers and bird feathers. The 2009 Horn of Plenty collection was his the last one. He himself described it as "A parody of the punk female ideal that does not exist [...] Everything is extreme, an illusion." This collection was a sarcastic condemnation of the recession that was just beginning to bite. McQueen had sensed how serious this would become and, in fact, he had the models walk around a pile of trash, as if they were in a dump, a metaphor of the times. But, because of his premature death in 2010, he never saw the show.

213 In his shows, the visionary and surreal designer Alexander McQueen always featured spectacular creations that were often imbued with Gothic, almost fetish overtones.

214 and 215 Among the most often used materials are leather and feathers that sometimes entirely covered his dresses, which were known for their classical forms, full skirts and tight-fitting bodices that produced surprising results.

216 and 217 The 2007 show featured models who seemed to arrive directly from the past, with waxen faces and gowns echoing fin de siècle opulence, hourglass lines and prominent hips.

218 and 219 Two designs from the 2008-2009 fall-winter collection. Their classical forms were embellished with details that gave them a surreal air, which was one of the characteristics of Alexander McQueen, who has been called the 'hooligan of Haute Couture'.

220 and 221 Two designs in the final fashion show designed by McQueen, entitled The Horn of Plenty, which was a denouncement of the imminent world economic crisis.

Sarah Burton

The regal and romantic 2011 spring-summer collection was the first one created by Sarah Burton, who, after fifteen years as British designer Alexander McQueen's assistant, became the creative director of his brand after he died, in February 2010. She also shares, and still renovates, the visionary stylist's sartorial skill and creativity, using the same features: sculptural forms, unusual materials, surreal prints and such decorative elements as feathers, leaves and butterflies for lavish evening gowns with a romantic flavor. And, during the 2011 collection show, the models wore dresses either covered with butterflies, in autumn colors, that flew off the garments, as if paying a final tribute to the great stylist, or covered with layers of voile that formed a sort of plant sculpture. One iconic creation was the ice-white gown with feathers that reminds one of the 18th-century dress-panniers, with a skin-tight bodice and broad shoulders, covered with white goose feathers. Indeed, the feathers on the skirt and the latter's loose quality gave the impression that the gown might have taken flight at any moment. On the other hand, the 2013-2014 fall-winter collection was inspired by various queens, from Marie Antoinette to Victoria: long dresses with loose balloon skirts and a cut reminiscent of the 18th and 19th century, and bustiers overlaid with pearls and gilded embroidery, a motif repeated in the metal net headdress. "I really think that creating clothes and fashion has to be a statement about how we live and where we live and what's happening in the world," Burton asserted. Alexander McQueen would probably be very proud to have left the reins of his fashion house to such a sensitive stylist, who is certainly capable of continuing his magical and surreal line and approach.

223 The Ice Queen and Her Court was the title of the 2011 show that celebrated regal and strong femininity, with touches of fetish typical of the McQueen style. This white gown was made with raw-edged layers of organza.

224 and 225 Lace masks cover the heads and parts of the faces of the models on the catwalk during the 2012 spring-summer fashion show. Much attention was paid to the fabrics, carefully worked and embellished with ruche, embroidery, pearls and paillettes. The forms of these designs remind one of Victorian attire.

"I really think that creating clothes and fashion has to be a statement about how we live and where we live and what's happening in the world."

Sarah Burton

226 A cocoon effect is achieved in this red gown made of layers of ruche and with a marked couture flavor.
It was part of the 2012-2013 fall-winter collection.

227 Detail of a mini-coat in the same collection, made of laser-cut leather. It has an hourglass silhouette and a Tibetan
goat-wool stole over the shoulders.

228 This pink dress was
made of layers of organza
with a radial cut, which
created an ovoid volume
made narrow at the waist
by a belt.

229 An equally
complicated, and
markedly sculptural,
creation was this
floor-length pink dress
consisting of numerous
tiny layers of fabric.

He is one of the most talented contemporary stylists who, despite his rather 'tender age' (he was born in 1980) already boasts an excellent track record, having founded his own fashion house in 2011. Posen is a favorite for his style, which draws from the past, from the masterful art of the great couturiers, while at the same time looks toward the future – with many of the elements that are identifiable with some of his predecessors, such as volant, ruche, folds, plissé, embroidery and decorative elements on constructed, architectural lines with well calibrated volumes and proportions. Posen's creations are similar to those of another major American tailor-stylist who lived a few decades before him, Charles James, known for his 'fruit clothing' made with such great sartorial skill that they almost seemed to be products of engineering. Without going so far, Posen's style is close to James's in its precise sartorial construction, in the use made of materials able to support lines that often resemble the famous Clover Leaf. These are siren lines whose upper part is in the shape of a bustier and whose skirts end in tails and trains, often with shimmering textures – such as in the splendid evening dresses in the 2012-2013 fall-winter collection – and colors ranging from beige to very bright yellows. Here mention must be made of the design worn by actress Lena Dunham at the 2014 Golden Globe ceremony. Other fine designs are the more tapering silhouettes embellished with sartorial details worthy of stylists such as Balenciaga, Balmain or Armani, with layers of volant, tulle and organza that make figures seem unreal and to have been transported directly from the past, when elegance was the benchmark that distinguished high society and when ready-to-wear was yet to be born.

"I'm not interested in trend, I am interested in timeless clothing."

Zac Posen

232 and 233 Posen's style reminds one of that of a top couturier of the past, Charles James, known for his architectural creations and his precise sartorial construction, with well-calibrated volumes – the very same features we find in this red gown. The bustier, with a heart-shaped neckline, becomes a taffeta and tulle 'maxi-skirt' that is made even more particular by the diagonal drapery.

234 For his spring-summer collection Zac Posen designed not only ample and theatrical designs, but also streamlined ones that ended in soft black silk chiffon skirts with purple leaf-like shapes.

235 This lurex top of a blue gown designed in 2012 is striking: a heart-shaped neckline overlaid with a crisscrossed swath of chiffon. The floor-length skirt is made of soft, flared cotton faille.

236 and 237 Sarah Bernhardt, the famous 19th-century actress, was the inspiration for Posen's 2014 spring-summer fashion show. These gowns, made of silver-colored mikado silk and with hourglass silhouettes, have a series of flounces on the hips and in the lower part of the skirt.

"In America my
role is to continue
a great tradition
of social dressing.
I even go so far
as to say there is
sensuality in the
cut and outfitting.
This is what keeps
a dress from being
dated and makes it
interesting."

Zac Posen

AUTHOR

MARIA MACCARI was born in Milan, earned her degree in Italian Literature, specializing in History of Costume and Fashion, and then got a Master's degree in New Technologies. She began a career in journalism almost by chance, beginning with a brief working experience with Mondadori Publishers. Since 2000 Ms. Maccari has been a web editor for Condé Nast, specializing in Beauty and Well-Being, and has also contributed to the creation of such sites as iosposa.it, style.it and vanityfair.it. Ms. Maccari is now engaged in launching a Glamour Beauty portal. She is an aficionado of cinema, art and history, and is also very interested in politics.

Cover

The fall-winter prêt-à-porter collection 2005-2006, presented in Paris, closes with a red silk evening gown bearing a train and a bow at the waist. A classic that carries the unmistakable signature of Valentino but nonetheless demonstrates a trend typical of that season: a taste for the Victorian Era.
© *Stephane Cardinale/People Avenue/Corbis*

Backcover

'Powdery' greys and pinks often become even more surprising and interesting thanks to the soft, flowing line of the fabric, as in this elegant design from Valentino's 2005 spring-summer haute couture collection.
© *Gamma-Rapho/Getty Images*

The Publisher would like to thank the Guccio Gucci S.p.A. and Maison Galitzine.

WS White Star Publishers® is a registered trademark
property of De Agostini Libri S.p.A.

© 2015 De Agostini Libri S.p.A.
Via G. da Verrazano, 15 - 28100 Novara, Italy
www.whitestar.it - www.deagostini.it

Translation: Richard Pierce
Editing: Norman Gilligan

ISBN 978-88-544-0944-6
1 2 3 4 5 6   19 18 17 16 15

Printed in China